The Silk Road

The **Complete Chinese** Cookbook

The Silk Road

The Complete Chinese Cookbook

NOTES

Standard level spoon measurements are used in all recipes.
1 tablespoon = three teaspoons

Eggs should be medium to large unless otherwise stated.
The U.S. Food and Drug Administration advises that eggs should
not be consumed raw. This book contains dishes made with raw or
lightly cooked eggs. It is prudent for pregnant women and
nursing mothers, invalids, the elderly, babies, and young children
to avoid uncooked or lightly cooked dishes made with eggs. Once
prepared, these dishes should be kept refrigerated and used
promptly.
Meats and poultry should be cooked thoroughly. To test if poultry
is cooked, pierce the flesh through the thickest part with a skewer
or fork — the juices should run clear, never pink or red. Do not
re-freeze poultry that has been frozen previously and thawed.
Do not re-freeze a cooked dish that has been frozen previously.

Use whole milk unless otherwise stated.

Nut and Nut Derivatives
This book includes dishes made with nuts and nut derivatives. It
is advisable for those with known allergic reactions to nuts and
nut derivatives and anyone potentially vulnerable to these
allergies, such as pregnant and nursing mothers, invalids, the
elderly, babies, and children to avoid dishes made with nuts and
nut oils. It is also wise to check the labels of pre-prepared
ingredients for the possible inclusion of nut derivatives.

Pepper should be freshly ground black pepper unless otherwise
stated.

Fresh herbs should be used, unless otherwise stated. If
unavailable, use dried herbs as an alternative, but halve the
quantities stated.

Ovens should be pre-heated to the specified temperature — if
using a fan-assisted oven, follow the manufacturer's instructions
for adjusting the time and the temperature. Oven temperatures
will need adapting by those living at high altitude.

Contents

Introduction

Chinese people are passionate about food. Chinese families spend hours gathered round the table, planning what they are going to eat, eating it, and then reminiscing about their favorite dishes and preferred cooking methods. But food is associated with much more than just delicious tastes and sustenance. Eating well is actually thought to be essential to living well.

When Chinese people meet each other, they say "Chi fan le mei yo?" which means, literally, "Haven't you eaten rice yet?" This is an everyday greeting, and is tantamount to saying "How are you?" in English. It also entails a wish for a person's good health and happiness.

Four schools of Chinese cookery

In China, there are an estimated 55 ethnic minorities, each of which has contributed something different to the many and varied culinary skills to be found in this vast country. It is hardly surprising, then, that there is no single Chinese way of cooking. There are, rather, a great many culinary traditions.

These can be grouped into the four main schools of Chinese cookery which depend largely on the climate and, in turn, on the availability of local produce.

The four main schools of Chinese cuisine are:
○ *Cantonese* ○ *Huaiyang* ○ *Szechuan* ○ *Beijing*

Cantonese

Cantonese cooking is found mostly in the Kwangtung province of China, which is in the south of China near Hong Kong. Cantonese food is probably the best known in the West, because many Chinese families emigrated from this area of China to Europe and America in the nineteenth century.

Cantonese cooking tends to be regarded as the haute cuisine of China. This probably harks back to the brilliant chefs of the Imperial Court, who fled to Guangzhou, or Canton, when the Ming dynasty was overthrown in 1644.

The Cantonese are keen on exotic delicacies, such as snake, frog's legs, and dog. Cantonese cooking also owes much to the ready availability of locally caught fish and seafood. There are therefore a great many seafood specialities. For example, vegetables are often filled with a seafood stuffing.

The Cantonese also love sweet-and-sour flavors. They are famous for their dumplings, one of the favorite *dim sum* delicacies, which are served as a light lunch or afternoon snack. The area has come to be known as one of the rice bowls of China and, not surprisingly, rice is the staple diet.

The Cantonese avoid heavy, overpowering flavors such as garlic and spices. They prefer, instead, to rely for their flavorings on the use of soy, hoisin, and oyster sauces, all of which help achieve a subtle blend of aromas and colors. Food is often slightly undercooked, which allows the natural flavors, textures, and colors to be preserved. Stir-frying and steaming are therefore the most popular cooking methods.

pork, poultry, and fish. Dishes that come from the Szechuan region tend to be richly flavored, spicy, even hot. This is largely due to the fiery chili peppers, hot pepper oil, and the Szechuan peppercorns, ginger, onions, and garlic, all of which are widely used in the area.

Beijing

Beijing (formerly known as Peking in the West) is not only the capital city of China, but also its culinary center, because chefs from all the different regions of the country gravitated to Beijing over the centuries, bringing with them specialities from their own particular area. Its cuisine therefore tends to be very varied.

Best known of all, perhaps, is the glorious dish still known by its old name of Peking Duck. This consists of succulent pieces of crispy duck served in steamed mandarin pancakes with plum sauce, green onions (scallions), and cucumber. This is an elaborate banquet dish, and was probably developed because the Imperial Court of China was based in the city. You will find the recipe for this superb dish on page 92.

This area is also famous for its sweet-and-sour dishes, which come from the northern province of Honan on the Hwang Ho River.

Beijing is in the north of China, where the climate can be harsh. Fresh vegetables are only available at certain times of the year, and people have therefore learned how to preserve foods to see them through the long, cold winters. Vegetables that store well, such as potatoes, turnips, and cabbages, are widely used, and preserved ingredients such as dried mushrooms and pickled fruits and vegetables are also popular.

Flavors tend to be strong, owing to the widespread use of garlic, leeks, onions, sesame seeds and oil, and sweet bean sauce.

Grains other than rice tend to be used as the staple

Huaiyang

Huaiyang cuisine is found mainly around Yangchow, on the eastern coast of China bordering on the East China Sea. The area possesses some of the most fertile land in China, and has a rich variety of fresh fruits and vegetables at its disposal. Not surprisingly, it is noted for its vegetarian cuisine. The area is dominated by the estuary of the Yangtze River, and the coastline is very long. Fresh fish and shellfish are therefore plentiful.

Specialities from this area include many steamed dishes, including the popular savory dumplings. There are also many noodle dishes, renowned for their subtle flavors, which hail from the Yangtze River delta.

Other regions of eastern China include Nanking, which is famous for its succulent duck recipes, and Shanghai, which has a rather more sophisticated cuisine of its own. Cooks in the East of China are particularly keen on stir-frying, steaming, blanching, and red-cooking (which means slow-simmering in dark soy sauce). The food has acquired a reputation for richness, because of its widespread use of oil and sugar in savory dishes.

Szechuan

This is the western region of China, which is entirely inland. Fruits and vegetables are easily available, as are ingredients. These include wheat, corn, and millet, which the northerners eat in the form of bread, noodles, dumplings, and pancakes.

Store pantry ingredients

There are many ingredients that you will find in your store pantry which will come in handy in Chinese cookery. Some of these are listed below.

Rice

There are many different types of rice, including long-grain, short-grain, and glutinous varieties. Brown rice is not used in China, where most people dislike its texture.

The most popular rice is long-grain white rice. Glutinous, or sticky, rice is a medium-grain rice which becomes sticky and sweet when boiled. It is widely used in baking and for dessert dishes. Despite its name, it is completely gluten-free!

Garlic

Chinese cookery relies on the use of garlic as an essential flavoring. Buy fresh garlic, which may be used whole, chopped, or crushed, and keep it in a cool, dry place. Garlic should not be kept too long in the refrigerator, it may become moldy or begin sprouting.

Oils

Oil is commonly used as a cooking medium. Peanut oil is pleasantly mild and is excellent for stir-frying and deep-frying. Safflower and sunflower oils are also good.

Sesame oil has a distinctive, nutty flavor and is often used in Chinese cookery. Be warned however — it is more commonly used as a seasoning than as a cooking oil because it tends to burn easily. Sesame oil is often added at the last minute to add flavor and to finish a dish.

Specialist ingredients

Authentic Chinese cooking is not possible without the use of certain specialist ingredients which add distinctive flavor and color. Specialist Chinese ingredients are easily available from supermarkets and Chinese food markets. Because so many Chinese live abroad, most major cities have their own Chinatown area, with colorful stores, restaurants, and food markets. Just browsing around them offers a fascinating glimpse into the rich diversity of the culture. Another excellent source of oriental ingredients is your nearest large supermarket. There is such interest in Chinese food nowadays that a good range of basic ingredients is available there. You will find special features throughout this book which supply detailed information about specialist ingredients.

Preparing the ingredients

Chinese cookery places the emphasis on preparing the ingredients rather than cooking them. There is a lot of cutting, chopping, dicing, and shredding involved, and this is the time-consuming part of the process as the cooking time is relatively short.

Cooking methods

Common methods of cookery including stir-frying, steaming, and red braising.

Stir-frying

This is the most common method of all, and entails simply frying foods in a small amount of oil over high heat, stirring constantly. This method ensures that the food is sealed and cooked very quickly, which allows it to maintain its flavor, texture, and color — all so important to the success of the finished dish. The key to this method involves having the ingredients ready before you start

cooking, which will take only minutes. Stir-fried foods must not be overcooked or greasy.

Steaming

This is a very healthy way of preparing foods, and again allows foods to hold their original flavor, color, and texture. It is particularly well suited to foods that have a delicate taste or texture, such as fish and vegetables.

Red-braising

This method of cooking is peculiar to China. It entails stewing food in a mixture of soy sauce, water, and sugar, with additional flavorings of root ginger, green onion (scallion), and rice wine. The food takes on a red tinge during the cooking process — hence the name. It is particularly well suited to tougher cuts of meat and certain vegetables that do not cook quickly.

Eating Chinese-style

The easy informality of Chinese eating makes mealtimes very relaxed and pleasurable. Rather than a set pattern of appetizer, entrée, and dessert, a selection of various dishes is set on the table. This does not mean that a Chinese meal is set out at random — the selection of dishes will be carefully chosen to complement each other, in order to achieve the ideals of balance and harmony. Contrasts of taste, texture, and color are very important.

Each guest has a bowl, chopsticks, and perhaps a decorative porcelain spoon for soup, and everyone helps themselves to the food.

One major advantage is that this means far fewer dishes to wash, as the same bowl can be used throughout the meal. If you wish to serve wine with your meal, try light fruity wines in both red or white varieties. If you prefer, you can serve tea — jasmine is extremely popular. A pretty oriental teapot is a nice touch, and these are easily available from Chinese stores.

Using a wok

A wok, with its specially rounded base and sloping sides, is the perfect piece of equipment for stir-frying. Its shape allows the heat to spread evenly over the surface which encourages rapid cooking, and its depth allows you to toss foods quickly without spilling them.

Choose a large wok with deep sides. The best ones are made of carbon steel, rather than stainless steel or aluminum, which tend to scorch. There are also nonstick woks available on the market, but these are more expensive and cannot be seasoned (see below,) which detracts from the flavor of the food that is cooked in them. To season a wok, scrub it first to remove the machine oil which is applied by the manufacturer to protect it in transit, and then dry it, and put it on the stovetop over a low heat. Add 2 tablespoons of cooking oil, and rub this all over the surface, using absorbent

paper towels. Heat the wok slowly for 10–15 minutes and then wipe with more paper. Repeat the coating, heating, and wiping process until the paper towels come away clean.

You should never need to scrub your wok again. Just wash in plain water and dry thoroughly by placing it over low heat for a few minutes before storing it. This will prevent your wok from rusting.

Accessories you may find useful with your wok include:
• a stand, which is a metal ring designed to keep the wok steady on the stovetop. It is essential if you want to use your wok for steaming, deep-frying, or braising.
• a lid, which is dome-shaped and absolutely essential if you use your wok for steaming. You can, of course, use any other sort of lid which fits snugly over the top of the wok or, failing that, you can use aluminum foil.
• a bamboo brush, which is a bundle of stiff, split bamboo and is used for cleaning the wok without scrubbing it.

Fresh broth recipes

You will find it very useful to refer to these basic recipes as they are required throughout the book.

A good broth is easy and cheap to make, with only a few basic ingredients. It is not necessary to resort to broth cubes, when the flavor of a fresh aromatic broth is far superior. For beef or fish broth you should be able to find the bones and trimmings you need at the market.

Once made, the broths can be frozen when cooled. Freeze in small batches in plastic tubs or ice cube trays. When frozen, the cubes can be transferred to clearly labeled plastic bags for ease of storage.

A few basic rules are necessary when making broth.
• Broth should always simmer extremely gently, or it will evaporate too quickly and become cloudy.
• Never add salt to the broth as simmering will reduce it and concentrate the flavor. This will affect the flavor of the finished dish.
• Any scum that rises to the surface should be removed as it will spoil the color and flavor of the final broth.
• Avoid any floury root vegetables as these will cause the stock to become cloudy.

Beef broth
• Put 5 pounds beef or beef and veal bones in a roasting pan, and place in a preheated oven at 450°F. Roast for 1 hour or until browned and the fat and juices run. Using a slotted spoon, transfer the bones to a large pot.
• Place the roasting pan on top of the stove, add 2 onions roughly chopped, 2 carrots roughly chopped, and 2 celery stalks roughly chopped. Fry gently in the remaining fat until nicely browned, but do not burn. Add the vegetables to the bones in the saucepan, together with 2 bay leaves, a few parsley stalks, 2 sprigs thyme, 10 whole peppercorns, and cover with 5 quarts cold water.
• Bring to the boil, skim any scum from the surface, reduce the heat and simmer, uncovered, for 8 hours, skimming occasionally. Strain and cool, then refrigerate. Remove any surface fat on the surface.

Makes about 11¼ cups
Preparation time: 5–10 minutes
Cooking time: about 9 hours

• Place 3 pounds fish trimmings and 1 onion, sliced, white part of a small leek, 1 celery stalk, 1 bayleaf, 6 parsley stalks, 10 whole peppercorns and 2 cups dry white wine into a large pot, and cover with 7½ cups cold water. Bring slowly to just below boiling point. Simmer for 20 minutes, removing any scum from the surface. Strain the broth through a cheesecloth-lined sieve and leave to cool before refrigerating.

Makes 7½ cups
Preparation time: 10 minutes
Cooking time: 20 minutes

Chicken broth

Chicken broth is used extensively in Chinese cooking, so a good recipe is essential. The following gives a light, delicately flavored broth which has a good flavor, but will not overpower the ingredients in the final dish.

• Chop a cooked chicken carcass into 3 or 4 pieces and place it in a large pot with the raw giblets and trimmings, 1 onion roughly chopped, 2 large carrots roughly chopped, 1 celery stalk roughly chopped, 1 bay leaf, a few parsley stalks, lightly crushed, and 1 sprig thyme. Cover with 7½ cups cold water.
• Bring to the boil, removing any scum from the surface. Lower the heat and simmer for 2–2½ hours. Strain the broth through a cheesecloth-lined sieve and leave to cool completely before refrigerating.

Makes 1 quart
Preparation time: 5–10 minutes
Cooking time: about 2½ hours

Fish broth

When purchasing fish bones and trimmings for this broth, avoid oily fish. It is very important that the broth does not boil or it will become cloudy.

Vegetable broth

This recipe makes a well-flavored vegetable broth which makes a good basis for many recipes, and can also be varied to your own taste. Once you have made it several times, you might wish to experiment with other flavorings. You can also ring the changes according to which vegetables are in season at the time. Try adding some fennel bulb for a mild aniseed flavor, or a sliver of orange zest for an added lift. The addition of tomatoes will give it richness of flavor and color. Avoid any floury root vegetables, however, as these will cause the broth to become cloudy.

• Place 2 cups chopped mixed vegetables, such as carrots, leeks, celery, onion, and mushrooms, about an equal quantity of each; 1 clove garlic, 6 peppercorns, 1 bouquet garni (2 parsley sprigs, 2 sprigs thyme, and 1 bay leaf) in a pan, and cover with 5 cups water. Bring to the boil and simmer gently for 30 minutes, skimming when necessary. Strain the broth and leave to cool completely before refrigerating.

Makes 1 quart
Preparation time: 5–10 minutes
Cooking time: about 45 minutes

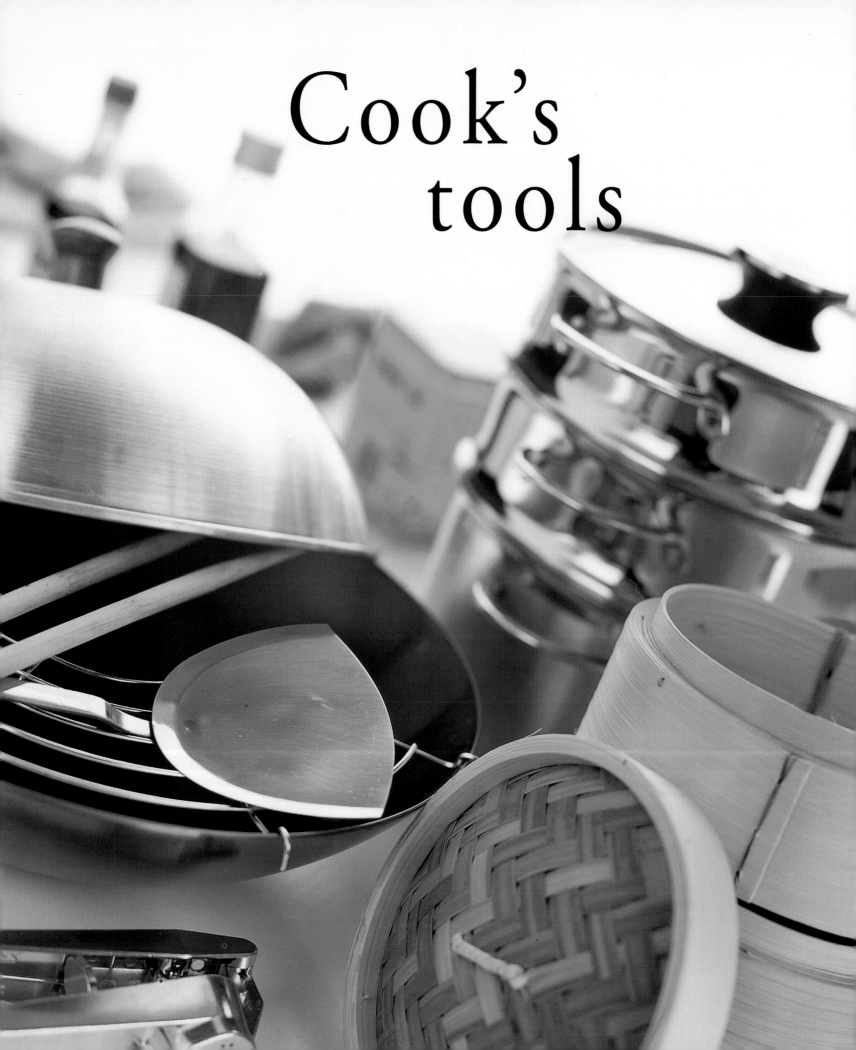

Cook's tools

Soups and Appetizers

Hot and Sour Soup
with shrimp and mushrooms

Szechuan pickled vegetables are used to give this soup its special, hot-sour flavor. They are readily available in Chinese supermarkets.

4 dried Chinese mushrooms
2 celery stalks
3¾ cups Chicken Broth (see page 11)
¾ cup bay shrimp, fresh or frozen, and thawed
¼ cup Szechuan pickled vegetables, sliced
¼ cup canned bamboo shoots, drained and shredded
½ cucumber
2 tablespoons Chinese wine or sherry
2 tablespoons soy sauce
1 tablespoon red wine vinegar
1 ounce ham, diced
1 green onion (scallion), chopped

soak the dried mushrooms in warm water for 15 minutes. Squeeze dry, discard the hard stalks, then slice the mushroom caps.

slice the celery stalks diagonally.

bring the broth to the boil, add the shrimp, pickled vegetables, bamboo shoots, mushrooms, and celery, and simmer for 5 minutes.

cut the cucumber into 2-inch matchstick lengths. Add them to the pan with the Chinese wine or sherry, soy sauce, vinegar, and ham, and cook for 1 minute.

sprinkle with the chopped green onion (scallion) and serve immediately.

Serves 4–6
Preparation time: *20 minutes*
Cooking time: *6–8 minutes*

Chicken Broth

with spareribs and shrimp

In China, the clear-simmering method is used to cook this delicate soup. It is traditionally made in an earthenware pot (called a sandpot) set over low charcoal heat.

1 meaty chicken carcass
1½ pounds pork spareribs
1 pound ham or beef bones
2 quarts water
2 teaspoons salt
2 teaspoons dried shrimp (optional)

put all the ingredients in a large, heavy pan or Dutch oven.

bring to the boil, cover, and simmer gently for 1¾ hours, skimming off any scum frequently.

leave to cool. When cold, skim any fat from the surface.

reheat and serve as a soup or use as required.

Serves 6
Preparation time: *15 minutes*
Cooking time: *1¾–2¼ hours*

clipboard: In the West, the clear-simmering technique can be achieved by cooking in a heavy, flameproof pot or Dutch oven over a very low heat or in a cool oven. Few flavoring ingredients are used during cooking, and this is preferred by many people, as they can then flavor their portion to taste. Spicy dips are usually served at the table to counteract the blandness of clear-simmered food. Sometimes clear-simmered foods are quickly deep-fried before serving.

Spicy Chicken Soup

with garlic, turmeric, and beanthread noodles

3 tablespoons sunflower oil
½ large onion, thinly sliced
2 garlic cloves, crushed
1 teaspoon fresh root ginger, chopped
½ teaspoon freshly ground black pepper
pinch of turmeric
¾ cup coarsely chopped cooked chicken,
1 tablespoon light soy sauce
1 quart Chicken Broth (see page 11)
a handful of beanthread noodles, soaked until soft
⅓ cup beansprouts
green onions (scallions), chopped, to garnish

heat the oil in a medium saucepan and fry the onion, garlic, and ginger until the onion is soft.

add the pepper, turmeric, and chicken and stir for 30 seconds.

add the soy sauce and broth and bring to the boil. Adjust the seasoning if necessary. Reduce the heat slightly and cook for 5 minutes.

drain the noodles. Divide them equally among 4 warmed soup bowls. Divide the beansprouts among the bowls and pour the soup on top.

serve hot, garnished with chopped green onions (scallions).

Serves 4
Preparation time: *15–20 minutes*
Cooking time: *15 minutes*

clipboard: Beanthread noodles, also called cellophane noodles, are made from mung bean flour. They must be soaked before cooking to make them soft.

Chicken and Sweetcorn Soup

with red pepper garnish

7¾ cups Chicken Broth (see page 11), with a little of the cooked chicken reserved and chopped
1½ cups sweetcorn kernels
2 teaspoons cornstarch (optional)
1 tablespoon water (optional)
salt and pepper

To garnish
green onions (scallions), chopped
or
½ red bell pepper, deseeded and chopped into dice and strips

pour the broth into a large saucepan and add 1 cup of the sweetcorn.

bring to the boil, add salt and pepper to taste, cover, and simmer for 15 minutes.

liquidize until smooth, then return to the pan.

reheat the soup. If it is not thick enough for your liking, blend the cornstarch with the water to make a thin paste, stir into the soup, and bring to the boil, stirring.

add the remaining sweetcorn and the reserved chopped chicken. Simmer for 5 minutes.

adjust the seasoning before serving, and garnish with the chopped green onions (scallions), or red bell pepper, if liked.

Serves 4
Preparation time: *10 minutes*
Cooking time: *20–25 minutes*

Sweetcorn and Fish Soup *with ginger and green onions*

1 pound white fish, such as cod or sea bass, filleted

1 teaspoon ginger juice, extracted from fresh root ginger (see clipboard)

1 teaspoon Chinese wine or sherry

3¾ cups water

1 x 8-ounce can sweetcorn, drained

1 teaspoon oil

1½ teaspoons cornstarch, dissolved in 1 tablespoon water

1 green onion (scallion), chopped, to garnish

salt

place the fish in a shallow heatproof dish with the ginger juice, Chinese wine or sherry, and a generous pinch of salt.

leave to marinate for 10 minutes.

place in a steamer and steam for 5–6 minutes. Remove from the heat and mash the fish with a fork. Set aside.

pour the water into a large saucepan and bring to the boil. Add the sweetcorn, oil, and 1 teaspoon of salt. Simmer for 2 minutes.

add the cornstarch mixture and cook, stirring, until the soup thickens.

add the fish and cook for 1 minute. Pour into soup bowls, sprinkle with green onion (scallion), and serve hot.

Serves 4–6
Preparation time: *15 minutes, plus 10 minutes marinating*
Cooking time: *about 15–20 minutes*

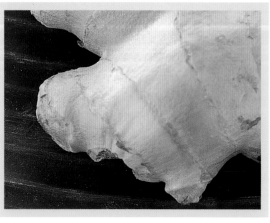

clipboard: Ginger juice can be extracted from the fresh root by placing small, peeled pieces in a garlic crusher, and squeezing firmly until you have the required amount.

Fish Soup
with coriander leaves

Fragrant coriander (cilantro) leaves — also known as Chinese parsley — add their pungent scent to this wonderfully aromatic fish soup.

8–12 ounces fish fillets, such as sole, halibut, cod, bream, bass, or carp, cut into 1½ x 1 inch slices
1 teaspoon salt
1 tablespoon cornstarch
3¾ cups Chicken Broth (see page 11)
2 slices root ginger, shredded
1 egg white, lightly beaten
3 tablespoons red wine vinegar
½ teaspoon pepper
1½ tablespoons coriander (cilantro) leaves, chopped

rub the fish slices with the salt and cornstarch.

bring the broth to the boil in a pan. Add the ginger, then taste, and add salt if necessary.

dip the fish slices in the beaten egg white, then add them to the broth, a few at a time.

return the broth to the boil, then reduce the heat, and simmer gently for 5 minutes, or until the fish is tender.

sprinkle the soup with the vinegar, pepper, and coriander (cilantro) leaves. Stir a few times, then transfer to a serving tureen. Serve hot.

Serves 4
Preparation time: *20 minutes*
Cooking time: *20–30 minutes*

clipboard: The use of a lightly seasoned chicken broth in this soup gives it a delicate flavor, so try to avoid using a bouillon cube if possible.

Shrimp and Squid Hot Soup

For a really warming, spicy start to a meal, there is nothing to beat this mouthwatering soup. It is packed with the aromatic flavors of lemongrass, chilies, and coriander

8 ounces squid, cleaned

7½ cups Chicken Broth (see page 11)

3 lime leaves

1 stem lemongrass, crushed

1 cup raw shrimp, peeled

nam pla, to taste

2–4 fresh chilies, deseeded, sliced into rounds

2 garlic cloves, crushed

juice of 1 lime or 1 lemon

coriander (cilantro) leaves, freshly chopped, to garnish

prepare the squid: hold the head and tentacles in one hand and pull away the body with the other. Pull the innards and the hard 'pen' away from the body and discard. Cut the tentacles from the head. Scrape the thin skin from the body and tentacles. Rinse well and pat dry. Cut the squid into rings.

put the broth, lime leaves, and lemongrass in a pan and bring to the boil. Reduce the heat and simmer for 5 minutes. Add the shrimp, squid, and *nam pla*. Cook until the shrimp turn pink. Add the chilies.

pour the soup into 4 warmed individual bowls. Combine the garlic and lime or lemon juice, and stir into the soup. Sprinkle with chopped coriander and serve hot.

Serves 4–6
Preparation time: *15 minutes, plus 10 minutes marinating*
Cooking time: *about 15–20 minutes*

clipboard: *Nam pla* is a salty, spiced, fermented fish mixture, available from oriental food stores.

Coin Purse Eggs
with fresh coriander

This Szechuan dish acquired its evocative name because the folded-over eggs are thought to resemble purses containing golden coins.

6 tablespoons sunflower oil

8 eggs

3 tablespoons light soy sauce

2 tablespoons white wine vinegar

4 tablespoons coriander (cilantro) or flat-leaved parsley, chopped (optional)

salt and pepper

heat 2 tablespoons of the oil in a skillet over a moderate heat. Break in 1 egg, moving the yolk to one side, if possible.

add salt and pepper. Fry until the underside is set. Fold over one side of the white to cover the yolk completely.

increase the heat and cook until the underside is golden brown. Turn the egg over carefully and brown the other side.

transfer the egg to a warmed serving dish and keep warm.

cook the remaining eggs in the same way.

combine the soy sauce and vinegar, and sprinkle this over the eggs. Scatter with the chopped herbs, if using, and serve with a stir-fried dish of your choice.

Serves 4
Preparation time: *5 minutes*
Cooking time: *15–20 minutes*

Green Peppers
stuffed with pork and ginger

1 tablespoon sunflower oil
1 garlic clove, crushed
1 piece fresh root ginger, peeled and finely chopped
1 cup lean ground pork
1 green onion (scallion), chopped
1 celery stalk, finely chopped
rind of 1 lemon, grated
4 green bell peppers

heat the oil in a wok or skillet over a moderate heat. Add the garlic and stir-fry until lightly browned.

reduce the heat and add the ginger and pork. Stir-fry for 2 minutes.

add the green onion (scallion), celery, and lemon rind. Combine well and stir-fry for another 30 seconds. Let the mixture cool slightly.

cut the peppers into quarters lengthwise and remove the core and seeds.

divide the mixture between the pepper quarters, pressing it down into each of the cavities.

arrange the pepper quarters in an oiled, ovenproof dish. Cook in a preheated oven at 400°F degrees for 25 minutes, until tender.

transfer to a warmed serving platter and serve immediately.

Serves 4-6
Preparation time: *15 minutes*
Cooking time: *30–35 minutes*
Oven temperature: *400°F*

clipboard: If you are using a new wok for the first time, you must remove the protective film of oil. Heat the wok over high heat until very hot, then scrub it with warm soapy water. Rinse and dry over moderate heat. Season the wok by wiping it with a pad of absorbent paper towels soaked in cooking oil. Wash without detergent after each use.

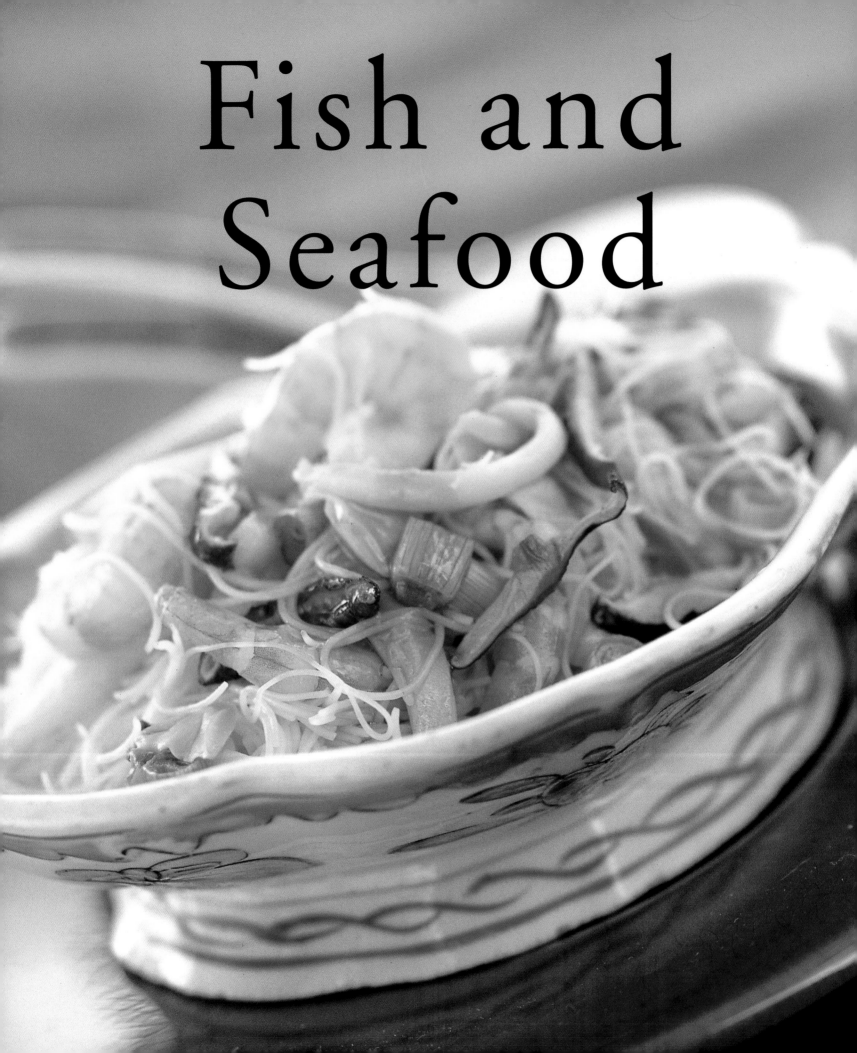

Fish and Seafood

Scallop and Shrimp
stir-fry with mixed vegetables

4–6 fresh scallops

½–¾ cup raw shrimp, heads removed, defrosted if frozen

1 egg white

1 tablespoon cornstarch

3 celery stalks, trimmed

1 red bell pepper, cored and deseeded

1–2 carrots, peeled

2 slices fresh root ginger, peeled

2–3 green onions (scallions)

2½ cups vegetable oil, for deep-frying

2 tablespoons Chinese wine or dry sherry

1 tablespoon light soy sauce

2 teaspoons chili bean paste (optional)

1 teaspoon salt

1 teaspoon sesame seed oil, to finish

cut each scallop into 3–4 pieces. Peel the shrimp and remove the black vein. Leave the shrimp whole if small, otherwise cut each one into 2 or 3 pieces. Put the seafood in a bowl with the egg white and about half of the cornstarch, and mix together.

cut the celery, red bell pepper, and carrots into small pieces. Finely shred the ginger and green onions (scallions).

heat the oil in a hot wok, then deep-fry the scallops and shrimp for 1 minute, stirring them all the time with chopsticks to keep the pieces separate. Scoop them out with a perforated spoon and drain on absorbent paper towels.

pour off all but 2 tablespoons of oil from the wok. Increase the heat to high and add the ginger and green onions (scallions). Add the vegetables and stir-fry for about 1 minute, then return the scallops and shrimp to the wok, and stir in the wine or sherry, soy sauce, and chili bean paste (if using). Season with the salt.

mix the remaining cornstarch to a smooth paste with a little broth or water, then add to the wok, and blend all the ingredients until thickened. Sprinkle with the sesame seed oil and serve immediately.

Serves 4–6
Preparation time: *20–25 minutes*
Cooking time: *6–8 minutes*

Szechuan Shrimp
in chili and tomato sauce

This is a typical Szechuan dish — hot, peppery and richly flavored with chili sauce.

1 cup raw shrimp, peeled
1 egg white
2 teaspoons cornstarch
sunflower oil for deep-frying
1 green onion (scallioin), minced
2 slices fresh root ginger, peeled and minced
1 garlic clove, minced
1 tablespoon Chinese wine or dry sherry
1 tablespoon tomato paste
1 tablespoon chili sauce
lettuce leaves
salt
tomato rose, to garnish (optional)

mix a pinch of the salt with the shrimp, add the egg white, and dust with cornstarch.

heat the oil in a wok or deep pan. Add the shrimp, stirring to keep them separate, and deep-fry for 30 seconds over moderate heat.

remove from the wok and drain.

pour off all but 1 tablespoon of oil from the wok. Over a high heat, stir-fry the green onion (scallion), ginger, and garlic for a few seconds.

add the shrimp and stir-fry for 1 minute. Add the wine, tomato paste, and chili sauce, stirring until the sauce is well blended.

line a dish with lettuce and pour the shrimp and sauce into the center. Serve immediately, garnished with a tomato rose, if liked.

Serves 4
Preparation time: *20–25 minutes*
Cooking time: *5 minutes*

clipboard: To make a tomato rose, remove the skin in one continuous strip about ½ inch wide. With the flesh side inside, curl it from the base end, forming a flower shape.

Deep-fried Shrimp Cutlets
in a light, crispy coating

8 jumbo shrimp
1 tablespoon Chinese wine or dry sherry
1 egg, beaten
2 tablespoons cornstarch
oil for deep frying
sprig of coriander (cilantro) (optional)

hold the shrimp firmly by the tail and remove the shell, leaving the tail shell piece intact.

cut the shrimp in half lengthwise almost through to the tail, and remove the dark intestinal vein.

flatten the shrimp with a light wooden mallet to resemble cutlets. Sprinkle with the Chinese rice wine or sherry.

dip the cutlets in beaten egg, then in the cornstarch, and then repeat. Heat the oil to 350°F.

deep-fry the shrimp for 2–3 minutes. Drain them thoroughly on absorbent paper towels.

arrange on a serving platter and garnish with fresh coriander (cilantro), if liked.
Serve plain or with sweet soybean paste.

Serves 2
Preparation time: *20 minutes*
Cooking time: *2–3 minutes*

clipboard: Rice wine is made from fermented rice and is sold in Chinese markets. You can use dry sherry as a substitute.

Scrambled Eggs
with shrimp and beansprouts

Crisp, firm beansprouts add texture to the fresh eggs and shrimp, making this a deliciously healthy, easy-to-prepare dish.

8 eggs

3 tablespoons soy sauce

4 tablespoons oil

2 medium onions, thinly sliced

1 garlic clove, finely chopped

⅔ cup beansprouts

½ cup shelled shrimp

beat the eggs with the soy sauce.

heat the oil in a wok or large skillet on a high heat.

put in the onions, garlic, and beansprouts and stir-fry for 1 minute.

mix in the eggs and the shrimp. Cook, stirring constantly, until the eggs set to a scramble.

Serves 4
Preparation time: *10 minutes*
Cooking time: *5–6 minutes*

clipboard: Beansprouts are the sprouts of small green mung beans. Although they are available in cans, it is best to use them as fresh as possible. They are widely available in supermarkets and grocery stores. You can grow your own beansprouts by putting some mung beans in a jar. Cover with a piece of cheesecloth and secure with an elastic band. Rinse the beans every day until the sprouts are long enough to eat.

Stir-fried Crab
with ginger and green onion

Fresh crabs are a favorite ingredient in Chinese cooking. If you are unsure about preparing them, you can ask for this to be done for you at the market.

1 x 1½-pound crab
2 tablespoons Chinese wine or dry sherry
1 tablespoon Chicken Broth (see page 11) or water
2 tablespoons cornstarch
4 slices fresh root ginger, peeled and finely chopped
4 green onion (scallions), finely chopped
3 tablespoons sunflower oil
1 teaspoon salt
1 tablespoon light soy sauce
2 teaspoons sugar

wash the crab shells and separate the legs and claws. Crack the claws.

crack the shells into 2–3 pieces. Discard the feathery gills, the black sac and the intestinal thread.

place the crab in a bowl with 1 tablespoon of the wine or sherry, the broth or water, and the cornstarch.

stir once or twice and leave to marinate for 10 minutes.

combine the chopped ginger and green onion (scallion).

heat the oil in a wok or frying pan until it is hot, then add the crab pieces and stir-fry for 1 minute.

add the ginger and onion, the salt, soy sauce, sugar, and remaining wine or sherry. Cook for about 5 minutes, stirring constantly.

add a little water if the mixture becomes very dry. Serve hot.

Serves 4
Preparation time: *25–30 minutes, plus 10 minutes marinating*
Cooking time: *6 minutes*

Quick-fried Crab

in aromatic oil with garlic

Because stir-frying is such a quick process, the cooking oil is often scented with aromatic flavorings first — with garlic and ginger, as in this recipe, or with chilies.

1 x 1½-pound crab, freshly cooked
2 tablespoons sunflower oil
1 clove garlic, crushed
2 pieces root ginger, finely chopped
4 green onions (scallions), chopped
1 leek, thinly sliced
1 egg, beaten
⅔ cup Fish Broth or Chicken Broth (see page 11)
2 tablespoons Chinese wine or dry sherry
2 teaspoons cornstarch, blended with 1 tablespoon water
salt
1 teaspoon sesame oil, to finish
lemon wedges, to garnish

break off the legs and crack the claws of the crab. Using a cleaver, crack the shell into 4–5 pieces.

remove all the meat and cut into pieces, discarding the black sac and intestinal thread.

heat the oil in a wok or frying pan, add the garlic, ginger, and green onions (scallions) and stir-fry for 1 minute.

add the crab and stir-fry for 5 minutes over a high heat. Add the leek and salt to taste.

lower the heat and pour in the egg in a thin stream. Add the broth and wine or sherry, and cook for 1 minute.

add the cornstarch and sesame oil; cook, stirring, until thickened.

turn onto a warmed serving platter and serve the crab immediately, garnished with lemon wedges.

Serves 4–6
Preparation time: *about 20 minutes*
Cooking time: *7–10 minutes*

Stir-fried Fish
with bacon and mixed vegetables

If you prefer, you can use any good quality, firm white fish in this recipe. Red snapper or haddock are excellent, for example. Check at the market to see what is available.

1 pound cod fillet, skinned and cut into wide strips
1 teaspoon salt
1 tablespoon oil
2 slices lean bacon, shredded
2 tablespoons cooked garden peas
2 tablespoons cooked sweetcorn kernels
6 tablespoons Chicken Broth (see page 11) or water
2 teaspoons Chinese wine or dry sherry
2 teaspoons light soy sauce
1 teaspoon sugar
1 teaspoon cornstarch
1 teaspoon water

To garnish
lemon slices (optional)
green onions (scallions)

sprinkle the fish fillets with the salt and leave to stand for 15 minutes.

heat the oil in a wok or skillet over a moderate heat.

add the fish and bacon and stir-fry for 3 minutes.

add the remaining ingredients, except the cornstarch and water, and bring to the boil.

blend the cornstarch with the water to make a thin paste and add to the sauce. Stir and cook for 1 minute.

serve hot, garnished with lemon slices, if using, and green onions (scallions).

Serves 4
Preparation time: *5 minutes, plus 15 minutes standing*
Cooking time: *5–7 minutes*

Mixed Seafood
with stick noodles and ginger

4 dried Chinese mushrooms

I pound rice noodles

2 tablespoons oil

4 green onions (scallions), chopped

2 garlic, cloves sliced

I piece root ginger, finely chopped

¼ cup frozen peeled shrimp, thawed

½ cup fresh or frozen squid, sliced (optional)

I x 8-ounce can clams, drained

2 tablespoons Chinese wine or dry sherry

I tablespoon soy sauce

salt

soak the mushrooms in warm water for 15 minutes. Squeeze well, discard the stalks, then slice the mushroom caps.

cook the rice stick noodles in boiling salted water for 7–8 minutes until they are just tender.

drain and rinse in cold water. Keep on one side.

heat the oil in a wok or deep skillet, add the green onions (scallions), garlic and ginger and stir-fry for 30 seconds.

stir in the mushrooms, shrimp, and squid, if you are using them, then cook for 2 minutes.

stir in the remaining ingredients, then carefully stir in the noodles and heat through.

pile the mixture into a warmed serving dish and serve immediately.

Serves 4–6
Preparation time: *10 minutes, plus 15 minutes soaking*
Cooking time: *10–11 minutes*

clipboard: Chinese dried mushrooms (shiitake) are strongly flavored, but they must be soaked for 15–20 minutes before using. They are available from Chinese markets. Shiitake are occasionally available fresh.

Stir-fried Squid
with green peppers and ginger

8 ounces squid
sunflower oil for deep-frying
2 slices fresh root ginger, peeled and thinly sliced
2 green bell peppers, deseeded and sliced
1 teaspoon salt
1 tablespoon light soy sauce
1 teaspoon wine vinegar
1 teaspoon sesame oil
pepper

prepare the squid: hold the head and tentacles in one hand and pull away the body with the other.

pull the innards and the hard "pen" away from the body and discard. Cut the tentacles from the head.

scrape the thin skin from the body and tentacles. Rinse well and pat dry. Cut the flesh into small pieces the size of a matchbox.

heat the oil over moderate heat in a wok or skillet and deep-fry the squid for about 30 seconds, stirring with chopsticks to prevent the pieces sticking together.

pour off all but 1 tablespoon of oil from the wok. Add the ginger, green peppers, and squid and stir-fry for 1 minute.

add the salt, soy sauce, vinegar, and pepper and stir-fry for 1 minute. Add the sesame oil and serve hot.

Serves 4
Preparation time: *20 minutes*
Cooking time: *about 5 minutes*

clipboard: If you do not wish to clean the squid yourself, you can buy it ready-prepared at the fresh fish counter of large supermarkets. It is certainly convenient to buy it this way if you do not have much time. Try to get the smallest squid available, as they will be the most tender.

Baby Squid
stir-fried with fresh, green herbs

2 pounds baby squid
4 tablespoons sunflower oil
3–4 garlic, cloves sliced
2 tablespoons coriander (cilantro), freshly chopped
1 tablespoon flat-leaved parsley, freshly chopped
juice of ½ lemon
salt and pepper

prepare the squid: hold the head and tentacles in one hand and pull away the body with the other.

pull the innards and the hard "pen" away from the body and discard. Cut the tentacles from the head.

scrape the thin skin from the body and tentacles. Rinse well and pat dry. Cut the flesh into slices. Season with salt and pepper to taste.

heat the oil in a wok over gentle heat. Add the garlic slices and cook until browned. Remove with a slotted spoon and discard.

increase the heat. When the oil is hot, add the squid, and cook briskly for 1 minute, stirring to prevent the pieces sticking together.

add the coriander (cilantro), parsley, and lemon juice and stir-fry for 30 seconds. Transfer to a warmed serving dish.

serve immediately, garnished with slices of lemon or lime, and tiny sprigs of fresh herbs.

Serves 4
Preparation time: *about 10 minutes*
Cooking time: *2–4 minutes*

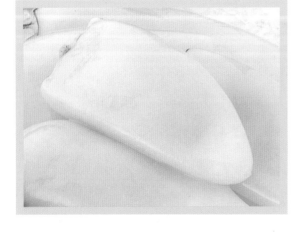

clipboard: Squid must be cooked quickly or the flesh becomes tough. Consequently, it is ideal for stir-fried dishes such as this. Baby squid is the best to use for stir-frying, as its flesh is delicate and very tender.

Braised Fish

with vegetables in black bean sauce

Colorful, fragrant, and fresh-tasting, this is a perfect way to prepare fish. The black beans make a wonderful sauce, and provide great color contrast.

3 tablespoons salted black beans
2 tablespoon oil
2 green onions (scallions), chopped
1 x 1-inch piece fresh root ginger, peeled and chopped
1 small red pepper, cored, deseeded, and chopped
2 celery stalks, chopped
2 tablespoons light soy sauce
2 tablespoons Chinese wine or dry sherry
4 x 5-ounce cod or haddock steaks
green onion (scallion), shredded, to garnish

soak the black beans in warm water for 10 minutes. Drain.

heat the oil in a wok or deep skillet. Add the green onions (scallions), ginger, red pepper, and celery and stir-fry for 1 minute.

stir in the soy sauce and wine or sherry. Place the fish on top of the vegetables and simmer for about 5–10 minutes, depending on the thickness of the fish. Cook until almost tender.

spoon over the black beans and cook for 2 minutes.

arrange the fish on a warmed serving dish and spoon the sauce over. Serve hot, garnished with shredded green onion (scallion).

Serves 4
Preparation time: *20 minutes*
Cooking time: *10–15 minutes*

clipboard: Black beans are salted and fermented, and have a very strong salty flavor. They are sold in plastic bags or cans in Chinese food stores, and will keep almost indefinitely, but they must always be soaked for 5–10 minutes before cooking.

Deep-fried Sole

with herbs and satay sauce

If possible, use Dover sole for this recipe, as it has a particularly fine flavor. It is expensive, and may be hard to find, so you may want to use lemon sole or flounder.

I teaspoon each of coriander, cumin,
and fennel seeds, crushed

2 garlic cloves, crushed

½ cup crunchy peanut butter

I teaspoon dark soft brown sugar

2 fresh green chilies, deseeded, chopped

⅔ cup coconut cream

2 cups water

3 tablespoons lemon juice

2 tablespoons butter

I shallot, minced

I tablespoon each of chives, tarragon
and parsley, chopped

grated rind of ½ lemon

8 Dover or lemon sole fillets

I egg, beaten

4–5 tablespoons fresh bread crumbs

sunflower oil, for deep-frying

sprigs of flat-leaved parsley, to garnish

make the sauce: heat a wok, add the spice seeds, and stir-fry for 2 minutes. Add the garlic, peanut butter, sugar, and chilies.

combine the coconut cream with the water and stir it in. Cook gently for 7–8 minutes. Stir in the lemon juice.

melt the butter in a skillet, add the shallot and cook for 1 minute. Stir in the herbs and lemon rind. Cool slightly.

pour this mixture over the fish fillets. Roll up each one and secure with wooden cocktail sticks.

dip in the egg, coat in bread crumbs, and deep-fry in hot oil for 4–5 minutes until golden.

drain and serve, garnished with a sprig of parsley, with the sauce handed separately.

Serves 4
Preparation time: *35 minutes*
Cooking time: *15–20 minutes*

clipboard: Coconut cream is sold in blocks, which should be softened in boiling water before use. Coconut powder, mixed to a paste with water, is an acceptable alternative.

Rainbow Trout
steamed in aromatic seasonings

What could be more delicious than these delicately flavored trout? Steaming is one of the healthiest ways to cook — no fat is required, and the taste of the food is perfectly preserved.

1 tablespoon sesame oil
1 tablespoon light soy sauce
1 tablespoon Chinese wine or dry sherry
2 rainbow trout, weighing about
2 pounds in total, cleaned
4 garlic cloves, sliced
6 green onions (scallions), shredded
1 x 2-inch piece fresh root ginger, peeled and shredded
2 tablespoons dry white vermouth
2 tablespoons sunflower oil

mix together the sesame oil, soy sauce, and wine or sherry and use to brush the inside and skin of the fish.

mix together the garlic, green onions (scallions), and ginger, and place a quarter of this mixture inside each fish.

place the fish on a heatproof plate, scatter with the remaining garlic mixture, and pour the vermouth and oil over it.

put the plate in a wok or steamer and steam vigorously for 15 minutes, or until the fish are tender.

arrange the cooked trout on a warmed serving dish, pour the juices over them, and serve at once.

Serves 4
Preparation time: *10 minutes*
Cooking time: *15–20 minutes*

clipboard: Traditional Chinese bamboo steamers are decorative as well as practical. They are designed so that they can be stacked on top of one another, allowing different foods to be steamed at the same time. They are available from Chinese supermarkets and cookware stores.

Fish Parcels
deep-fried and wrapped in paper

4 x 4 ounce fillets of sole or plaice
pinch of salt
2 tablespoons Chinese wine or dry sherry
I tablespoon vegetable oil
2 tablespoons green onion (scallion), shredded
2 tablespoons fresh root ginger, shredded
extra vegetable oil, for deep frying
green onion (scallion) tassels, to garnish

cut the fish fillets into 1-inch squares. Sprinkle with the salt and toss them in the wine or sherry.

cut out 6-inch squares of parchment paper or nonstick baking paper and brush them lightly with the oil.

place a piece of fish on each square of paper and arrange some shredded green onion (scallion) and ginger on top.

fold the pieces of paper into envelopes, tucking in the flaps firmly to secure them.

heat the oil in a wok or deep saucepan to 350°F or until a cube of day-old bread browns in 30 seconds. Deep-fry the wrapped fish parcels for 3 minutes.

drain and arrange on a warmed serving dish. Garnish with green onion (scallion) tassels and serve at once. Each person at the table unwraps their own fish parcels with chopsticks.

Serves 4
Preparation time: *15 minutes*
Cooking time: *3–5 minutes*

clipboard: Green onion (scallion) tassels are a popular Chinese garnish. Trim a 3-inch piece of the green stalk. Reserve the white bulb for another use. Finely shred the top leaves, leaving 1-inch attached at the base. Immerse in iced water until the tassel opens out and curls.

Fish Steaks
with soy sauce and ginger

Choose a robust white fish with a firm texture for this dish, as it will combine well with the rich, dark color and pungent flavor of the soy sauce.

1 pound fish steak, such as cod, halibut, monkfish, or hake
½ teaspoon salt
2 tablespoons Chinese wine or sherry
4 tablespoons cornstarch
1 egg white, lightly beaten
3 tablespoons sunflower oil
1 slice fresh root ginger, peeled and finely chopped
2 tablespoons light soy sauce
2 teaspoons sugar
½ cup Chicken Broth (see page 11) or water
green onion (scallion), to garnish

cut the fish steak into pieces about the size of a matchbook.

mix together the salt, wine or sherry, and 1 tablespoon of the cornstarch, and marinate the fish in this mixture for about 30 minutes.

dip the fish pieces in egg white, then in the remaining cornstarch.

heat the oil in a wok or skillet until hot, then fry the fish pieces until golden, stirring them gently to separate each piece.

add the ginger, soy sauce, sugar, and broth or water. Cook for 3–4 minutes, or until the liquid has completely evaporated.

serve hot, garnished with green onion (scallion).

Serves 4
Preparation time: *about 15 minutes, plus 30 minutes marinating*
Cooking time: *15–20 minutes*

clipboard: This method of coating fish in egg white and cornstarch before putting it in the hot oil is an excellent way of preventing the fish from breaking up during stir-frying.

Young Spinach
with clams and mustard sauce

Next time you find small, fresh clams at the market, try this Chinese method of cooking them. It is a perfectly delicious recipe for this familiar shellfish.

1 tablespoon Chinese wine or dry sherry
1 cup baby clams, cleaned
3 tablespoons soy sauce, plus 1 teaspoon
hot mustard
6 cups tender young spinach leaves,
washed and trimmed
salt
1 tablespoon sesame seeds, to garnish

heat the rice wine or sherry in a small saucepan. Add the clams and heat through. Drain, reserving the liquid.

mix 3 tablespoons of the soy sauce in a bowl with the mustard, then add the cleaned clams.

blanch the spinach leaves in lightly salted boiling water for 30 seconds. Drain and immediately plunge the leaves into a bowl of ice-cold water.

drain the spinach again and squeeze out any excess water. Pour 1 teaspoon soy sauce over it.

add the reserved liquid to the clam mixture. Arrange the spinach on a serving platter.

place the clam mixture in the center and garnish with sesame seeds. Serve at once.

Serves 4
Preparation time: *15 minutes*
Cooking time: *about 5 minutes*

clipboard: Sorrel or rocket are good alternatives to spinach, but if you use them, they need not be blanched.

Sauces

Hoisin sauce

Black bean sauce

Yellow bean sauce

Chili sauce

Light soy sauce

Yellow bean sauce
Yellow bean sauce is made from yellow soybeans. It is more of a paste than a sauce, and very similar in taste to soy sauce. Sold in bottles, it is sometimes used as a substitute for soy sauce, as it is thicker, and produces a richer sauce in cooking. Yellow bean sauce is now easily available in large supermarkets.

Black bean sauce
Black bean sauce is a thick, black sauce made from black soybeans. It can be used by itself as a savory dip or incorporated into stir-fried, braised, or fish dishes. Black bean sauce is easily made at home — a quick method is to blend sugar, garlic, and soy sauce to taste, together with a rinsed can of salted black beans.

Chili sauce
Chili sauce is a rich red sauce with a hot spicy taste. It is made from red chilies and can be used with all types of Chinese cooking either by itself or as a dip. Mostly it is sparingly incorporated into a dish, but chili sauce is used generously in Szechuan cooking, which is renowned for its hot, spicy dishes.

Light soy sauce
Light soy sauce has a delicate, mildly salty flavor, and is distinctly lighter in color than traditional soy sauce.
The color of any sauce is dependent on the length of time that it has been aged. Soy sauce is used in Chinese cooking, in seafood dishes, soups, and also as a dipping sauce.

Hoisin sauce
One of the most commonly used Chinese sauces is hoisin, a marinating sauce. It is used for broiling and barbecuing, and is also served separately as a dipping sauce. It is made from soybeans, tomato paste, and spices. Hoisin sauce is best known for its use with Chinese barbecued spare ribs.

Spices

Szechuan pepper

Five-spice powder

Star anise

Cinnamon

Cloves

Chili powder

Star anise
Star anise is the dried, star-shaped pod of a variety of magnolia tree, native to southern China. This attractively shaped spice is widely used in Chinese cooking, as its strong aniseed flavor complements various foods, especially meats and poultry.

Star anise is one of the spices used in five-spice powder.

Chili powder
Chili powder is dark red in color and is used in spicy dishes for its hot and peppery flavor. Depending on the type of chili used, it can vary considerably in strength so it is a good idea to be careful when adding it to food. You might try tasting a tiny portion on the tip of the finger to get an idea of its strength.

Szechuan pepper
Szechuan pepper is also known as Chinese pepper, but it is not a true pepper. These are the dried berries of a Chinese shrub. The pepper is very fragrant and has a strong, distinctive flavor, although it is not very hot. The berries are roasted prior to grinding. It is another ingredient in five-spice powder.

Cinnamon
Cinnamon is a light brown spice, with a strong, sweet aroma. It is frequently used in soups, baking, liqueurs, and flavored oils.

Five-spice powder
Five-spice powder is a fragrant mixture, and a traditional ingredient in Chinese cooking. In fact, the powder is often a mixture of more than five spices, but the main ingredients are star anise, Szechuan pepper, cinnamon, cloves, and fennel seeds.

Cloves
Cloves are the dried buds of a tropical evergreen. Their fragrance is fruity with a slightly bitter note. They are used in sweet and savory dishes.

Chicken and Poultry

Sweet Chicken Wings *braised with oyster sauce and ginger*

1 pound chicken wings

3 tablespoons oyster sauce

1 tablespoon soy sauce

1¼ cups Chicken Stock (see page 11)

pinch of salt

1 teaspoon brown sugar

2 tablespoons minced root ginger

pinch of black pepper

1 teaspoon coarse salt

green onion (scallion), finely sliced, to garnish

put the chicken wings into a pan with just enough cold water to cover.

bring to the boil, cover, and simmer for 10 minutes.

drain and discard the water.

put the chicken wings back into the pan and add the oyster sauce, soy sauce, broth, salt, and sugar.

bring slowly to the boil, cover and simmer for 20 minutes.

sprinkle the ginger, pepper, and coarse salt over the chicken. Serve hot, garnished with fine strips of green onion (scallion).

Serves 4
Preparation time: *10 minutes*
Cooking time: *30 minutes*

clipboard: Oyster sauce is widely used in Chinese cooking to flavor poultry, meat, and vegetables. Used mainly in the South of China, it is made from an extract of oysters and soy sauce. Oyster sauce is sold in bottles at Chinese foodstores and in most large supermarkets.

Stir-fried Lemon Chicken *with vegetables*

12 ounces chicken off the bone, skin removed
2 tablespoons Chinese wine or dry sherry
4 green onions (scallions), chopped
1 x 1-inch piece fresh root ginger,
peeled and minced
2 tablespoons sunflower oil
1–2 garlic cloves, sliced
2 celery stalks, sliced diagonally
1 small green bell pepper, cored, deseeded
and sliced lengthwise
2 tablespoons light soy sauce
juice of ½ lemon
rind of 2 lemons, shredded
¼ teaspoon chili powder

To garnish (optional)
lemon slices
sprig of parsley

cut the chicken into 3-inch strips. Mix the wine or sherry with the green onions (scallions) and ginger.

add the chicken and toss well to coat the pieces. Set aside to marinate for 15 minutes.

heat the oil in a wok or skillet and add the garlic, celery, and green pepper. Stir-fry for 1 minute.

add the chicken in its marinade and cook for a further 2 minutes.

stir in the soy sauce, lemon juice and rind, and the chili powder, and cook for 1 minute more.

transfer to a warmed serving dish and garnish with lemon slices and a sprig of fresh parsley, if liked.

Serves 4
Preparation time: *5 minutes, plus 15 minutes marinating*
Cooking time: *4 minutes*

Stir-fried Chicken
with shiitake mushrooms

2 tablespoons dried shiitake mushrooms
5 tablespoons sunflower oil
2 garlic cloves, crushed
8 ounces boneless chicken breast,
cut into strips
¼ cup baby corn cobs, blanched
¾ cup Chicken Broth (see page 11)
1 tablespoon *nam pla* (fish sauce)
generous pinch of salt
generous pinch of sugar
½ tablespoon cornstarch
2 tablespoons water

soak the dried mushrooms in warm water to cover for 5 minutes. Discard the stems and cut the caps into quarters.

heat the oil in a wok or large skillet. Add the garlic and cook over moderate heat until golden.

add the chicken and stir-fry for 10 minutes. Lift out and set aside.

add the mushrooms and baby corn to the oil remaining in the wok. Stir-fry 1-2 minutes.

stir in the chicken broth and bring to the boil. Reduce the heat, return the chicken to the wok, and season with *nam pla*, salt, and sugar.

simmer for 10 minutes or until the chicken is tender and the liquid is reduced by about half.

mix the cornstarch with the water to make a thin paste. Add to the chicken mixture and cook, stirring constantly, until the sauce thickens. Serve immediately.

Serves 4
Preparation time: *15 minutes, plus 5 minutes soaking*
Cooking time: *30 minutes*

clipboard: Dried shiitake mushrooms are sold in small packages at oriental food stores. They have an earthy, highly concentrated flavor, and are therefore used in small quantities.

Stewed Chicken
with chestnuts and ginger

Chicken has a special compatibility with the flavor of sweet chestnuts, as this recipe shows.

6 tablespoons soy sauce

1 tablespoon Chinese wine or dry sherry

1 x 2-pound chicken, boned and cut into 1½-inch pieces

2 tablespoons oil

2 slices root ginger, minced

4 green onions (scallions), minced

1 pound sweet chestnuts, peeled and skinned

2 cups water

1 tablespoon sugar

mix together the soy sauce and wine or sherry in a dish and add the chicken. Leave to marinate for 15 minutes.

heat the oil in a large pan. Add the chicken mixture, ginger, and half the green onions (scallions). Stir-fry until the chicken is golden.

add the chestnuts, water and sugar. Bring to the boil, cover, and simmer for 40 minutes or until tender.

serve hot, garnished with the remaining green onions (scallions).

Serves 3–4
Preparation time: *10 minutes, plus 15 minutes marinating*
Cooking time: *50 minutes–1 hour*

clipboard: If fresh sweet chestnuts are not available, canned or dried ones may be used instead. Canned chestnuts should be drained and added to the chicken mixture 10 minutes before the end of the cooking time. If dried sweet chestnuts are used, they should be soaked in warm water overnight before using, then cooked as for fresh chestnuts.

Braised Chicken
with red peppers and ginger

3 tablespoons oil

3 red bell peppers, cored, deseeded, and sliced into rings

1 teaspoon salt

2 tablespoons water

1 pound chicken meat, cut into 1-inch pieces

2 tablespoons minced root ginger

pinch of brown sugar

2 teaspoons Chinese wine or dry sherry

1 teaspoon cornstarch

2 teaspoons soy sauce

heat 1 tablespoon of the oil in a pan. Add the pepper rings and salt.

stir-fry for 1 minute, then add the water, and simmer gently until the liquid has evaporated.

remove the peppers from the pan and set aside.

heat the remaining oil in the pan. Add the chicken and ginger, and stir-fry for 1 minute. Stir in the sugar and wine or sherry.

dissolve the cornstarch in the soy sauce and add to the pan. Simmer, stirring, until thickened.

add the pepper rings and cook for 1 minute. Serve hot.

Serves 4
Preparation time: *15 minutes*
Cooking time: *40 minutes*

clipboard: Chinese recipes often require finely chopped root ginger. Here is a useful technique for doing this. Peel the piece of root, and trim both ends flat. Stand on one end, and make a line of vertical cuts with a sharp knife. Holding the cut root together, turn it at right angles. Cut through again, making lines of fine strips. These can then be neatly chopped into small squares.

Steamed Chicken
with bok choy

1 x 3-pound chicken
2 teaspoons salt
6–8 dried shiitake mushrooms
3 cups bok choy
5 slices fresh root ginger, peeled
2 chicken bouillon cubes
coriander leaves, to garnish

bring a large saucepan of water to the boil. Add the salt and immerse the chicken in the water. Skim off all scum that rises to the surface and boil for 5–6 minutes. Drain the chicken.

soak the mushrooms in boiling water and leave to stand for 20 minutes. Drain and discard the stems. Cut the cabbage into 2-inch slices.

place the mushrooms caps and ginger in a large, deep, heatproof bowl. Put the chicken on top of the vegetables and pour in just enough water to cover it. Cover the top of the bowl tightly with aluminum foil.

place the bowl in a large saucepan of water, which should not come more than halfway up the sides of the bowl.

bring the water to the boil, then simmer for 1 hour, topping up with boiling water if necessary.

lift out the chicken. Place the sliced cabbage in the bottom of the bowl and sprinkle with the crumbled bouillon cubes.

replace the chicken. Tightly cover the bowl again with aluminum foil and simmer gently for 1 more hour.

arrange on a warmed platter, and garnish with coriander, if liked.

Serves 4–6
Preparation time: *10 minutes*
Cooking time: *2¼–2½ hours*

Cashew Chicken
with garlic, wine, and ginger

A good example of how Chinese cooking orchestrates ingredients into perfect harmony, this is a popular classic dish.

12 ounces boneless chicken
1 egg white, lightly beaten
4 tablespoons Chinese wine or dry sherry
2 teaspoons cornstarch
3 tablespoons sunflower oil
4 green onions (scallions), chopped
2 garlic cloves, chopped
1 x 1-inch piece fresh root ginger, peeled, and finely chopped
1 tablespoon light soy sauce
½ cup unsalted cashew nuts

cut the chicken into ½-inch cubes. Mix together the egg white, half the wine or sherry, and the cornstarch.

place the chicken cubes in this mixture and toss until evenly coated.

heat the oil in a wok. Then add the green onions (scallions), garlic, and ginger, and stir-fry for 30 seconds.

add the chicken and cook for 2 minutes.

pour in the remaining wine or sherry and the soy sauce and stir well.

add the cashew nuts and cook for a further 30 seconds. Serve at once.

Serves 4
Preparation time: *5 minutes*
Cooking time: *3–4 minutes*

clipboard: Cashew nuts are widely used in Chinese cooking, and are highly prized for their sweet, rich flavor. As with other kinds of nuts, they are mostly used in chicken or in stir-fry vegetable dishes. Cashew nuts are very nutritious and are full of vitamins and minerals.

Ginger Chicken
with baby mushrooms

1½ pounds chicken breasts, cut into finger-sized pieces
1 teaspoon sugar
4 tablespoons sesame oil
1 x 4-inch piece fresh root ginger, peeled and finely sliced
about ⅓ cup water
1 cup button mushrooms
2 tablespoons brandy
2 teaspoons cornstarch, blended with 3 tablespoons water
1 teaspoon light soy sauce
salt and pepper

sprinkle the chicken with the sugar and leave to stand for 20–30 minutes. Season with salt and pepper.

heat the oil and sauté the ginger for 1 minute.

add the chicken pieces and cook for 3 minutes.

stir in the water and mushrooms. Cover and cook for a further 5 minutes, or until the chicken is tender.

add the brandy, cornstarch mixture, and soy sauce. Bring to the boil, stirring, until thickened. Serve at once.

Serves 4
Preparation time: *10 minutes, plus 20–30 minutes standing*
Cooking time: *10–15 minutes*

clipboard: Fresh ginger is required so often in Chinese cooking, it is worth keeping some on hand. It freezes very well — store it in plastic wrap, or in a small freezer bag. You can use the amount you need, and return the rest to the freezer. Ginger can also be kept in the refrigerator in a tightly sealed jar of dry sherry. Ground ginger is not an acceptable substitute for the real thing.

Spicy Chicken
braised with coconut juice

2 tablespoons oil

I x 2-pound chicken, cut into serving pieces

I tablespoon Chinese wine or dry sherry

2 tablespoons soy sauce

I teaspoon salt

pinch of pepper

2 onions, cut into quarters

3 green onions (scallions), chopped

3 garlic cloves, chopped

2 tablespoons curry paste

2 teaspoons curry powder

1¼ cups water

3 medium potatoes, cut into 1-inch pieces

2 medium carrots, cut into 1-inch pieces

4 tablespoons coconut juice

2 tablespoons all-purpose flour

2 teaspoons sugar

a few strips of green bell pepper, to garnish

heat 1 tablespoon of the oil in a skillet. Add the chicken and stir-fry until lightly browned.

add the wine or sherry, soy sauce, salt, and pepper. Stir-fry for 2 seconds, then add the onions. Stir-fry for 30 seconds, then transfer the mixture to a saucepan.

heat the remaining oil in the pan. Add the green onions (scallions) and garlic, and stir-fry for 1 second. Add the curry paste and curry powder.

stir-fry for 30 seconds, then stir in the water. Pour this sauce over the chicken and add the potatoes and carrots.

bring to the boil, cover, and simmer for about 20 minutes, or until the chicken is tender.

combine the coconut juice with the flour and sugar, and stir into the pan. Cook, stirring, until the sauce is thickened.

serve hot, garnished with strips of green pepper.

Serves 4
Preparation time: *15 minutes*
Cooking time: *30–40 minutes*

clipboard: This dish (and various other versions of it) is very popular in Singapore — so, though delicious, it is not a mainland Chinese recipe. A few drops of Tabasco or chili sauce may be added with the curry paste to enhance the hot flavor, if liked.

Stir-fried Turkey
in a sweet-and-sour sauce

Turkey breast is becoming a popular choice for a quick, easy meal. Cooked with this exquisite sweet-and-sour sauce, it has a great flavor.

Sauce
1½ tablespoons light soy sauce
1 heaping tablespoon tomato paste
2 teaspoons cornstarch
1¼ cups water
3 tablespoons unsweetened pineapple juice
2 tablespoons wine vinegar
1 heaping teaspoon brown sugar

Stir-fry
1 tablespoon sunflower oil
1 onion, finely chopped
1 turkey breast, skinned and cut into cubes
½ yellow or red pepper, cored, deseeded and sliced
3 mushrooms, sliced
green onion (scallion), to garnish

make the sauce: place all the ingredients in a small pan and mix well.

bring to the boil, then simmer, stirring, until thickened. Keep warm.

heat the oil in a wok and stir-fry the onion for 2 minutes. Add the turkey and stir-fry for 2–3 minutes.

add the pepper and mushrooms and cook for 2–3 minutes.

transfer to a warmed serving dish and pour over the sauce. Garnish with green onion (scallion) and serve hot.

Serves 4
Preparation time: *6 minutes*
Cooking time: *6–10 minutes*

clipboard: This is a perfect recipe to use with the convenient packs of turkey breasts that are widely available in supermarkets. Turkey breast meat is healthily low in fat and calories, and has a more pronounced flavor than chicken. Turkey used to be a special occasion meat for holidays — now it is an everyday ingredient.

Peking Duck

Probably the most famous of all Chinese dishes, this was first served in 1864 at the Chuan Chu Te restaurant. It is now simply called the Peking Duck restaurant!

1 x 4–4½-pound oven-ready duck
2 tablespoons soy sauce
2 tablespoons dark brown sugar

Mandarin pancakes
1 quantity of dough for mandarin pancakes (see page 238)

To serve
1 small cucumber, cut into 2-inch matchstick pieces
1 bunch green onions (scallions), cut into 2-inch matchstick pieces
8 tablespoons hoisin sauce
green onion (scallion) tassel (see page 62)

immerse the duck in a pan of boiling water for 2 minutes, then drain thoroughly. Hang up the duck to dry in a well ventilated room overnight. Mix together the soy sauce and sugar, and rub this over the duck.

hang for 2 hours or until the soy and sugar coating is completely dry. Place the duck on a rack in a roasting pan and cook in a preheated oven at 400°F for 1½ hours.

make the pancakes in the meantime (see method on page 238) and set them aside, keeping warm in a very low oven.

cut off all the crispy skin from the duck and arrange on a warmed serving dish. Garnish with cucumber.

remove all the meat and arrange on another warmed serving dish. Garnish with green onion (scallion). Place the hoisin sauce in a small bowl. Garnish the pancakes with a green onion tassel.

each diner prepares his/her own pancake. Spread hoisin sauce over a pancake, cover with a piece of duck skin and meat, top with cucumber.

Serves 4–6
Preparation time: *1 hour, plus hanging overnight and for 2 hours the following day*
Cooking time: *1½ hours*
Oven temperature: *400°F*

Eight-Treasure Duck *with ham, shiitake mushrooms, and bamboo shoots*

1 x 4-pound oven-ready duckling
2 tablespoons dark soy sauce
⅔ cup glutinous rice
1 cup water
4–5 dried shiitake mushrooms
1 tablespoon dried shrimp
2 tablespoons sunflower oil
2 green onions (scallions), minced
2 slices fresh root ginger, minced
½ cup bamboo shoots, cubed
½ cup diced, cooked ham
1½ teaspoons salt
1 tablespoon light soy sauce
2 tablespoons Chinese wine or sherry

brush the duck skin with the soy sauce. Cook the rice in the water following the package instructions. Prepare the mushrooms. Soak the shrimp in warm water for 20 minutes and drain.

heat the oil in a wok and stir-fry the green onions (scallions) and ginger for 30 seconds. Add the remaining ingredients, blend well, and extinguish the heat. Add the cooked rice and mix together all the ingredients.

pack this mixture into the duck cavity and close up the tail opening securely. Bake the duck on a wire rack in a pan in a preheated oven at 400°F for 30 minutes.

reduce the heat to 350°F for a further 45 minutes.
Spoon the stuffing out of duck on to the center of a dish. Cut the duck into neat pieces and arrange round the edge.

Serves 4–6
Preparation time: *35–40 minutes*
Cooking time: *1¼ hours*
Oven temperature: *400°F, then 350°F*

clipboard: The name of this dish refers to the number of favored ingredients used for the stuffing. Eight is regarded as an auspicious number for complete balance and harmony.

Stir-fried Duck

with bamboo shoots and almonds

The Chinese simply adore the rich taste and luscious texture of duck. This stir-fry is a simple but succulent way of cooking it.

1 pound lean duck meat
2 slices root ginger, shredded
1 garlic clove, crushed
3 tablespoons sesame oil
3–4 dried Chinese mushrooms (optional)
4 green onions (scallions), sliced
½ cup canned bamboo shoots, drained and sliced
3 tablespoons soy sauce
2 tablespoons Chinese wine or sherry
2 teaspoons cornstarch
2 tablespoons flaked almonds, toasted

cut the duck meat into small chunks and place them in a bowl with the ginger and garlic.

pour 1 tablespoon of the oil over the meat and marinate for 30 minutes.

soak the mushrooms in warm water for 15 minutes, if using. Squeeze dry, discard the hard stalks, then slice the mushroom caps.

heat the remaining oil in a wok or deep skillet, add the green onions (scallions), and stir-fry for 30 seconds.

add the duck and cook for 2 minutes. Add the mushrooms, bamboo shoots, soy sauce, and wine or sherry, and cook for 2 minutes.

blend the cornstarch with 1 tablespoon water and stir into the pan. Cook for 1 minute, stirring, until thickened. Stir in the almonds and serve.

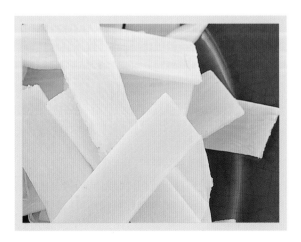

Serves 4–6
Preparation time: *15 minutes, plus 30 minutes marinating and 15 minutes soaking*
Cooking time: *6–7 minutes*

Braised Duck
with shiitake mushrooms

4 dried shiitake mushrooms

I x 4-pound duck, cut into individual portions

5 tablespoons light soy sauce

4 tablespoons sunflower oil

3 green onions (scallions), minced

4 slices fresh root ginger, peeled and minced

3 star anise

I teaspoon black peppercorns

2 teaspoons Chinese wine or dry sherry

½ cup canned bamboo shoots, drained and sliced

2 tablespoons cornstarch

2 tablespoons water

star anise to garnish (optional)

soak the mushrooms in boiling water for 20 minutes. Drain and discard the stems.

rub the duck with a little soy sauce. Heat the oil in a wok or large frying pan and fry the duck until it is golden all over. Transfer the duck to a saucepan, add the green onions (scallions), ginger, star anise, peppercorns, wine or sherry, remaining soy sauce, and enough cold water to cover.

bring slowly to the boil, reduce the heat and simmer for 1½–2 hours. Add the mushrooms and bamboo shoots 20 minutes before the end of the cooking time.

mix the cornstarch with the water and stir this mixture into the pan. Continue to cook until the sauce is thickened. Transfer to a warmed serving dish and serve hot, garnished with star anise, if liked.

Serves 4
Preparation time: *20 minutes, plus 20 minutes soaking*
Cooking time: *about 2½ hours*

clipboard: This dish can be started a day in advance. Simmer for 1½ hours, and leave to cool completely. Next day, skim off all excess fat, bring back to the boil, and add the mushrooms and bamboo shoots. Simmer for 20 minutes and finish as above. Star anise is a Chinese spice with a distinctive licorice flavor, shaped like a star with 8 points.

Barbecued Duck
with ginger and sesame seeds

4 boneless duck breasts, skin removed

Marinade
2 tablespoons brown sugar
I teaspoon salt
4 tablespoons light soy sauce
I tablespoon sesame oil
I x ½ inch piece fresh root ginger,
peeled and finely chopped
I teaspoon sesame seeds

cut the duck breasts into 32 evenly-sized pieces.

mix the marinade ingredients in a large bowl and add the duck.

stir, cover and marinate for 3–4 hours in a cool place or overnight in the refrigerator. Spoon the marinade over the duck several times, making sure that you coat the pieces evenly.

remove the duck with a slotted spoon and thread on to 8 bamboo skewers or 4 large metal skewers.

place the skewers on the grid of a moderately hot barbecue and cook the small skewers for 8–10 minutes, the larger ones for 10–12 minutes.

turn the skewers several times during cooking and baste with the remaining marinade.

serve the barbecued duck hot or cold, either on or off the skewers.

Serves 4
Preparation time: *20–25 minutes,*
plus 3–4 hours marinating
Cooking time: *8–12 minutes*

clipboard: You should be able to find pre-packed, ready-prepared duck breasts on sale at the poultry counter of larger supermarkets. They are excellent for stir-fries, or for barbecuing, as in this recipe.

Roast Squab *in a honey, soy, and garlic glaze*

4 oven-ready squab
¾ cup rice alcohol or vodka

prepare the squab by rubbing them inside and out with rice alcohol or vodka. Place on a wire rack and set aside to dry.

Marinade

5 tablespoons sunflower oil
3 garlic cloves, crushed
½ onion, finely chopped
2 tablespoons light soy sauce
2 tablespoons honey or dark corn syrup
⅓ teaspoon five-spice powder
pinch of freshly ground black pepper
6 tablespoons water

combine all the ingredients for the marinade.

paint the squab with this mixture inside and out, and leave to dry for 1 hour, either on a rack in a cool, well-ventilated room or preferably hanging by their necks.

brush the squab with the remaining marinade and roast on a rack in a pan in a preheated oven at 450°F for 20 minutes.

Lemon dip

2 lemons, cut in quarters
2 teaspoons salt
freshly ground black pepper

strip the flesh from the cooked squab and arrange on a warmed plate.

divide the lemon wedges among 4 dinner plates and add ½ teaspoon salt and a pinch of pepper to each.

make the dip: Each person makes their own dip by mixing the salt and pepper and moistening the mixture with a squeeze of lemon juice.

Serves 4
Preparation time: *30 minutes, plus 1 hour standing*
Cooking time: *20 minutes*
Oven temperature: *450°F*

clipboard: Squab are widely used in Chinese cooking, usually braised or deep-fried. *The secret of success is that the squab are marinated first to tenderize the flesh and to keep it from drying out.*

Special equipment

Wok

Garlic press

Colander

Wok

The wok is the most essential item in Chinese cooking, and many other kitchen tools are designed to work in conjunction with it. The wok is both hard-working and versatile. The round-bottomed design with sloping sides ensures that food can be deep-fried or stir-fried quickly, whilst using the minimum of oil. The wok's surface is also a good heat conductor. With a few basic accessories, food can be steamed, braised, or smoked, as well as stir-fried. Woks usually come complete with a steaming rack, and with a domed lid for steaming and braising. In addition, you will need a stand with sloping sides to place over the stovetop. This holds the wok in place at the heat source. Before using a wok for the first time, it should be thoroughly cleaned with detergent. Thereafter, simply wash it in hot water.

Garlic press

A garlic press is a very useful kitchen tool. The garlic is forced through a series of very small holes, allowing the oils to escape, and releasing the full flavor of the garlic. It protects your skin from the pungent aroma of the oil, and can also be used to extract juice from ginger.

Colander

The colander is used for separating liquids and solids and for draining and rinsing

Sieve

Stainless steel steamer

Measuring spoon

foods. Although they come in many shapes and sizes, colanders are basically bowls punched through with holes. They are usually made of plastic or stainless steel. The latter is much more practical as it is heat-resistant, dishwasher-proof, and hard wearing.

Sieve

A sieve has a rigid frame and a mesh body, whose gauge may vary from fine to coarse. It is used for separating solids from liquids, solids from solids, and also for refining ingredients. The mesh should be stainless steel to prevent rust.

Measuring spoon

Measuring spoons come in sets of a tablespoon, a teaspoon, half teaspoon, and a quarter teaspoon. They are available in aluminum, plastic, or stainless steel and are used for measuring both dry and liquid ingredients. When measuring liquids the spoons are filled to the top. For dry ingredients they should be leveled off. The same applies to measuring cups.

Stainless steel steamer

The stainless steel steamer performs the same function as the bamboo steamer, though the latter is often used in multiple layers. Stainless steel is certainly more practical to maintain and clean, and it lasts a lot longer than bamboo. Both are good at maintaining the flavor of the finished dish.

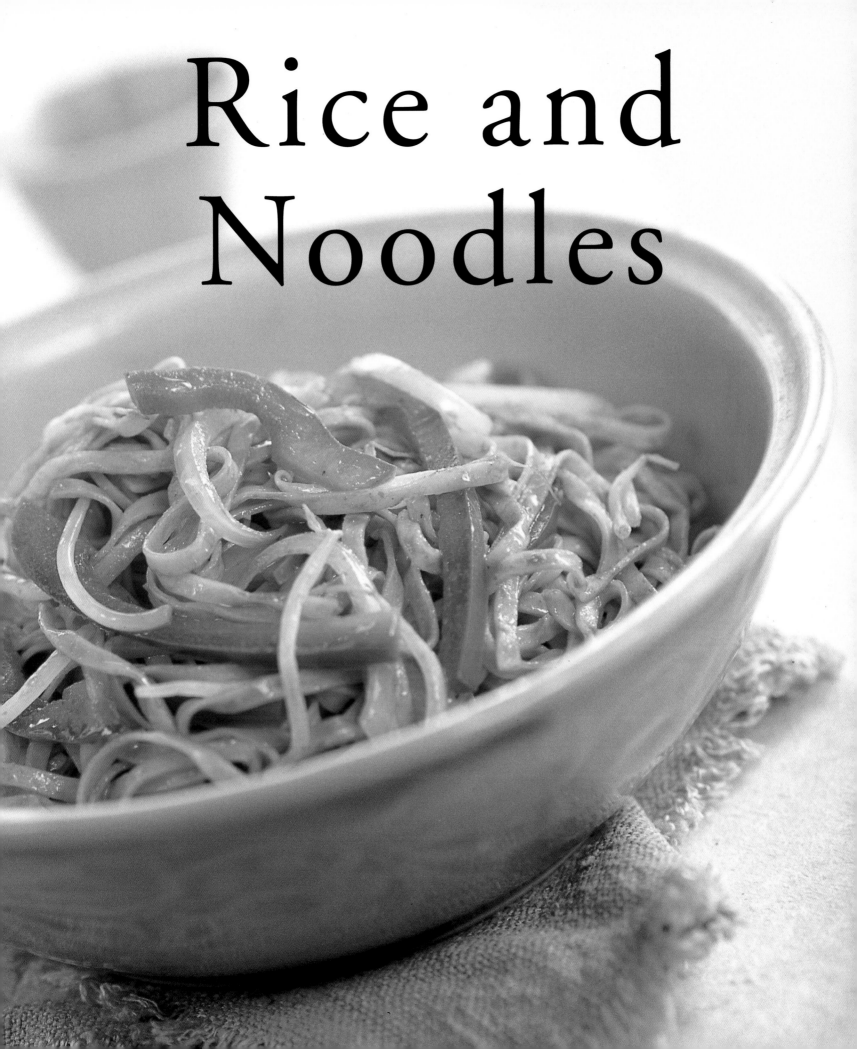

Rice and Noodles

Egg Noodles
in yellow bean and chili sauce

Egg noodles are mainly eaten in northern China. Marco Polo is reputed to have brought the recipe for pasta home to Italy after his travels in China, but this is now largely discounted as a myth, since noodles were eaten by the ancient Romans.

12 ounces Chinese egg noodles
3 tablespoons yellow bean paste
2 teaspoons chili sauce
1 garlic clove, crushed
3 tablespoons oil
2 green bell peppers, cored and deseeded
1 medium onion, thinly sliced
⅔ cup beansprouts
salt

cook the noodles in boiling, salted water for 5 minutes, or until it is just firm to the bite (*al dente*). Drain.

mix together the yellow bean paste, chili sauce, and garlic.

heat the oil in a wok or large skillet on a high heat. Put in the peppers, onion, and beansprouts and stir-fry for 2 minutes.

add the noodles and stir in the sauce mixture.

heat through and transfer to a warmed serving dish.

Serves 4
Preparation time: *10 minutes*
Cooking time: *10 minutes*

clipboard: Bean sauces are popular flavorings in Chinese cooking — yellow bean sauce is milder than black bean sauce. It is made from salted soybeans, garlic, soy sauce, vinegar, sugar, and seasoning.

Fresh Noodles
with sesame paste sauce

Fresh noodles are available at Chinese food stores, and are particularly delicious. Here they are flavored with an aromatic sesame sauce in a hot broth.

I pound fresh noodles

3¾ cups Chicken Broth (see page 11)

Sauce

2 tablespoons sesame seed paste

4 tablespoons water

4 tablespoons green onions (scallions), chopped

I teaspoon soy sauce

2 teaspoons red wine vinegar

2 teaspoons chili oil

I teaspoon salt

cook the noodles in plenty of boiling, salted water until just tender. Bring the broth to the boil in another pan.

make the sauce: mix the sesame seed paste with the water, then add the remaining ingredients.

when the noodles are cooked, drain well. Divide the boiling broth between four individual soup bowls.

add the cooked noodles and top with the sauce. Each person tosses the contents of his/her bowl before eating.

Serves 4–6
Preparation time: *10 minutes*
Cooking time: *10–15 minutes*

clipboard: Sesame paste is a favorite ingredient in Chinese sauces. It is quite similar to peanut butter, and has a very rich and aromatic flavor. Chili oil is available at Chinese food stores — you only need a small bottle as it should be used very sparingly.

Singapore Noodles

This is one of many versions of the tasty noodle dish sold by Singapore street hawkers. You can create your own variations, of course, but this one makes a really good late supper dish.

2 "nests" dry noodles

2¼ cups water

4 ounces lean pork, cut into 2-inch strips

⅓ cup raw shrimp, shelled

⅓ cup squid, cleaned and sliced

4 tablespoons sunflower oil

2 garlic cloves, crushed

⅓ cup beansprouts

1 tablespoon light soy sauce

1 tablespoon dark soy sauce

½ teaspoon freshly ground black pepper

1 bunch fresh chives, chopped

2 eggs

boil the noodles in plenty of water for 2 minutes. Drain.

bring the measured water to the boil in a pan and cook the pork, shrimp, and squid together for 5 minutes. Drain and reserve the liquid.

heat the oil in a wok or skillet and fry the garlic until golden. Add the beansprouts and noodles, increase the heat, and stir-fry for 2 minutes.

add the pork, shrimp, and squid, the soy sauces, pepper, and chives and stir-fry for 1 minute more.

push the mixture to one side of the pan and crack in the eggs. Cook for 1 minute and add the reserved liquid.

bring to the boil and cook for 2 minutes, stirring well. Transfer to a warmed serving dish and serve at once.

Serves 4
Preparation time: *15 minutes*
Cooking time: *14–18 minutes*

clipboard: Dried rice-stick noodles are sold at supermarkets and Chinese food stores. These convenient packages resemble little nests, so they are easy to recognize.

Crispy Fried Noodles *with spinach, chicken, and shrimp*

3 celery stalks
3 cups spinach
1 pound egg noodles or fettuccine
1 tablespoon oil
1 clove garlic, sliced
1 piece root ginger, minced
3 green onions (scallions), minced
4 ounces lean pork, sliced
4 ounces boned chicken breast, shredded
1 tablespoon soy sauce
1 tablespoon Chinese wine or dry sherry
¼ cup frozen peeled shrimp, thawed

slice the celery stalks diagonally and shred the spinach.

cook the noodles or fettuccine in boiling, salted, water according to the package instructions, until just tender. Do not overcook.

drain and rinse with cold water.

heat the oil in a wok or deep skillet. Add the garlic, ginger, and green onions (scallions) and fry for 1 minute.

add the pork and chicken and stir-fry for 2 minutes. Add the noodles, soy sauce, wine or sherry, and shrimp, and cook for 3 minutes.

pile on to a warmed serving platter and serve immediately.

Serves 4–6
Preparation time: *15 minutes*
Cooking time: *15–20 minutes*

clipboard: Chinese noodles are satisfyingly versatile in that they can be boiled and then stir-fried. When you use this method, make sure that they are *barely* tender before stir-frying, as over-cooking spoils their texture and makes them slightly sticky.

Tossed Noodles
with pork and vegetables

This is the sort of savory, aromatic noodle dish that transfers well to a modern, hectic lifestyle. It is full of interesting flavors, cooked in minutes, and makes a satisfying supper.

2 tablespoons oil
2 green chili peppers, deseeded, thinly sliced
1 clove garlic, thinly sliced
1½ cups ground pork
2 carrots, cut into matchstick lengths
3 celery sticks, cut into matchstick lengths
½ cucumber, cut into matchstick lengths
4 green onions (scallions), sliced
1 small green bell pepper, cored, deseeded and sliced
1 tablespoon soy sauce
2 tablespoons sweet red bean paste
1 tablespoon Chinese wine or dry sherry
12 ounces Chinese noodles, cooked

heat the oil in a wok or deep skillet, add the chilies and garlic, and fry quickly for about 30 seconds.

add the pork and cook for 2 minutes. Increase the heat, add the vegetables, and cook for 1 minute.

stir in the soy sauce, bean paste, wine or sherry, and Chinese noodles. Stir well to mix and heat through.

pile on to a warmed serving platter and serve immediately.

Serves 4–6
Preparation time: *10 minutes*
Cooking time: *5 minutes*

Transparent Noodles *with pork and black bean paste*

4 ounces transparent noodles
1 cup lean ground pork
1 teaspoon cornstarch
2 tablespoons light soy sauce
1 tablespoon hot black bean paste
½ cup Chicken Broth (see page 11) or water
4 tablespoons sunflower oil
4 green onions (scallions), minced
1 fresh green chili, deseeded and minced

soak the noodles in warm water for 10 minutes. Drain. Mix the pork with the cornstarch and soy sauce.

combine the bean paste with the broth or water.

heat the oil over high heat in a wok or large frying pan. Add the pork and stir-fry for about 2 minutes until it has browned.

stir in the noodles, green onions (scallions), chili and finally, the bean paste mixture.

bring to the boil and stir for about 1 minute, until all the moisture has evaporated.

transfer to a warmed serving dish and serve immediately.

Serves 4
Preparation time: *10 minutes, plus 10 minutes soaking*
Cooking time: *4–5 minutes*

clipboard: Transparent noodles, also known as beanthread or cellophane noodles, are used here to add bulk to a stir-fry, which makes a delicious and filling, one-pot dish.

Chow Mein

Literally translated, this means "stir-fried noodles" and was created by Chinese immigrants in America. It is so versatile that you can use whatever ingredients you have available.

1 pound Chinese egg noodles
4 tablespoons vegetable oil
1 medium onion, peeled and thinly sliced
4 ounces cooked meat (pork, chicken, or ham)
cut into thin shreds
½ cup snow peas or green beans
¼ cup fresh beansprouts
1 teaspoon salt
2–3 green onions (scallions), thinly shredded
2 tablespoons light soy sauce
1 tablespoon sesame seed oil or chili sauce, to finish
salt for boiling

cook the Chinese noodles in a large saucepan of boiling, salted water according to package instructions.

drain and rinse under cold running water until cool, and set aside.

heat about 3 tablespoons of the oil in a hot wok, add the onion, meat, snow peas or green beans and the beansprouts, and stir-fry for about 1 minute.

add 1 teaspoon salt and stir a few times more, then remove from the wok with a perforated spoon and keep hot.

heat the remaining oil in the wok and add the green onions (scallions) and the noodles, with about half of the meat-and-vegetable mixture.

mix with the soy sauce, then stir-fry for 1–2 minutes, or until completely heated through.

transfer the mixture from the wok to a warmed, large serving dish, then pour the remaining meat-and-vegetable mixture on top as a dressing.

sprinkle with the sesame seed oil or chili sauce (or both, if preferred). Serve immediately.

Serves 4
Preparation time: *15 minutes*
Cooking time: *15–18 minutes*

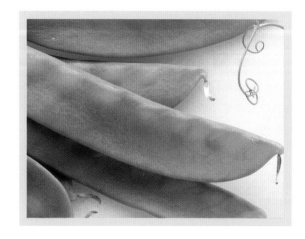

Chicken Chop Suey *with garlic*

2 tablespoons oil
5 green onions (scallions), chopped
1-inch piece root ginger, peeled and chopped
2 garlic cloves, crushed
6 ounces chicken breast, skinned
and cut into thin strips
1 tablespoon tomato paste
2 tablespoons Chinese wine or dry sherry
2 tablespoons soy sauce
1 teaspoon sugar
8 tablespoons water
1¼ cups beansprouts
3 eggs, beaten with 2 tablespoons water

heat 1 tablespoon of the oil, add the green onions (scallions) and ginger, and stir-fry for 1 minute.

add the garlic and chicken, and stir-fry for 2 minutes. Lower the heat, add the tomato paste, wine or sherry, soy sauce, sugar, and 5 tablespoons of the water.

heat through gently, then transfer to a warmed serving dish.

heat 2 teaspoons of the oil in the pan, add the beansprouts and remaining water, and stir-fry for 3 minutes.

add to the serving dish and keep warm.

wipe out the pan and heat the remaining oil. Pour in the beaten eggs and cook until set and crisp.

place on top of the beansprout mixture and serve at once.

Serves 4
Preparation time: *8 minutes*
Cooking time: *8–10 minutes*

clipboard: The term Chop Suey comes from the Chinese word *zasui* which means "mixed bits". Small portions of meat, fish, and vegetables can be thrown in, so you can use up leftovers. Do try and use at least one fresh vegetable, however, to give a crisp, fresh flavor to the dish.

Fried Rice
with ham and beansprouts

If you have leftover cooked rice, this is a great way to use it. You can prepare all the ingredients in advance, and stir-fry them just before serving.

2 tablespoons sunflower oil
2 green onions (scallions), finely chopped
1 garlic clove, crushed
1½ cups cooked long-grain rice
6 ounces cooked ham, diced
2 tablespoons light soy sauce
2 eggs
1 cup beansprouts, rinsed and drained
salt and pepper

heat the oil in a wok or skillet over moderate heat and stir-fry the green onions (scallions) and garlic for 2 minutes.

add the cooked rice next and stir well. Cook gently, stirring continuously, as the rice heats through.

stir in the ham and soy sauce. Beat the eggs thoroughly, with salt and pepper to taste.

pour into the rice mixture in a thin stream, stirring all the time.

add the beansprouts and continue cooking, stirring until all the ingredients are hot and the eggs are set. Serve at once.

Serves 4
Preparation time: *15 minutes*
Cooking time: *8–10 minutes*

clipboard: You don't need to use Chinese ham for this recipe — ordinary boiled ham is perfectly suitable.

Spicy Fried Rice
with red chili peppers

Chili fans will adore this dish, but it also tastes good made with sweet paprika or mild chili powder instead, and the color will be just as attractive.

1½ cups long-grain rice
2 cups water
2 tablespoons sunflower oil
4 shallots or 1 onion, thinly sliced
2 fresh red chilies, deseeded and thinly sliced
2 ounces chopped pork, beef or bacon
1 tablespoon light soy sauce
1 teaspoon tomato paste
salt

To garnish
a few slices of fried onion
1 plain omelet, made with 1 egg, cut into strips
a few fresh coriander (cilantro) leaves
a few cucumber slices

cook the rice (see Plain Boiled Rice page 132) and keep hot.

heat the oil in a wok or skillet, add the shallots and chilies, and fry for 1–3 minutes.

add the meat or bacon and fry for 3 minutes, stirring constantly.

add the rice, soy sauce, and tomato paste, and stir-fry for 5–8 minutes, then season with salt to taste.

transfer to a warmed serving platter and garnish with the onion, omelet, coriander (cilantro), and cucumber. Serve at once.

Serves 4
Preparation time: *15 minutes*
Cooking time: *about 25–30 minutes*

clipboard: A large selection of fresh chilies can be used in this dish. When preparing chili peppers, always wear rubber gloves. Remember that the seeds are the hottest part. Slit the chili lengthwise down the center, rinse under cold running water, and rub off the seeds. When handling chilies, don't put your fingers near your eyes, as the pungent juices will irritate and sting them.

Cantonese Rice

with shrimp, meat, and fresh mixed vegetables

1 cup long-grain rice, cooked
½ cup shrimp
2 teaspoons salt
1 egg white, lightly beaten
2 tablespoons cornstarch
1 pig's kidney, halved and trimmed
1 chicken liver, finely sliced
½ cup green beans, halved
3 tablespoons sunflower oil
2 green onions (scallions), cut into short lengths
4 ounces roast pork, finely sliced
4 ounces white fish fillet, cubed
1 teaspoon sugar
2 tablespoons light soy sauce
4 tablespoons Chicken Broth (see page 11)

cook the rice (see Plain Boiled Rice, page 132) and keep hot.

put the shrimp in a bowl with a pinch of salt, the egg white, and 1 tablespoon of cornstarch, and toss to coat.

score the surface of each kidney half in a crisscross pattern, then cut each half into 6–8 pieces.

blanch the shrimp, kidney, liver, and green beans in boiling water for 10–15 seconds, and drain.

heat the oil in a wok or skillet and stir-fry the green onions (scallions) briefly.

add all the meats, fish, and vegetables, with salt to taste, the sugar, and soy sauce. Stir-fry for 1 minute.

combine the remaining cornstarch with the broth and add to the wok, stirring. Serve on a bed of rice.

Serves 4
Preparation time: *30 minutes*
Cooking time: *30–35 minutes*

Special Rice

wrapped in lotus leaves

This dish lives up to its exotic name as it is delicately perfumed by the lotus leaf wrapping.

¾ cup long-grain rice, cooked
1 tablespoon sunflower oil
1 garlic clove, crushed
3 green onions (scallions), chopped
1 cup button mushrooms, sliced
2 ounces cooked ham, diced
4 ounces cooked chicken, diced
1 tablespoon garden peas
¼ cup canned bamboo shoots, drained and chopped
2 tablespoons light soy sauce
2 tablespoons Chinese wine or dry sherry
8 lotus leaves

cook the rice (see Plain Boiled Rice page 132) and keep hot. Soak the lotus leaves in warm water for 30 minutes. Drain thoroughly.

heat the oil in a wok or deep skillet, add the garlic and green onions (scallions), and stir-fry for 1 minute.

add all of the remaining ingredients except the lotus leaves, and continue cooking for 2 minutes. Cut each lotus leaf into 2 or 3 pieces and divide the mixture evenly among them.

fold the leaf sections to enclose the filling like a parcel, and secure with string. Place in a steamer and steam vigorously for 15–20 minutes.

pile the parcels onto a warmed serving dish and serve immediately, so everyone can open their own parcels.

Serves 4–6
Preparation time: *20 minutes, plus 30 minutes soaking*
Cooking time: *30–35 minutes*

clipboard: Dried lotus leaves are used for wrapping foods, but when fresh they can add a distinct flavor to dishes. If you can't find them, use one grape leaf for each parcel instead.

Plain Boiled Rice

In China, rice is an almost sacred symbol of life itself. It is so important that it is considered very bad luck to tip over or break a rice bowl.

I cup medium grain rice
2½ cups cold water
I teaspoon salt

put the rice, water, and salt into a saucepan. Set on a moderate heat and bring to the boil.

stir, then cover and simmer for 15 minutes or until all the water has been absorbed.

tip the rice into a colander or large sieve. Rinse under cold water to stop the cooking process.

rinse under hot water to clear any stickiness.

unmold the rice onto a wide, flat platter and leave in a warm place for about 5 minutes to dry.

fluff the rice with a fork twice during the drying time to separate the grains and ensure even drying.

Serves 4
Preparation time: *5 minutes, plus 5 minutes standing*
Cooking time: *15–20 minutes*

clipboard: Medium- and short-grain rice are generally preferred in Chinese cooking, as the cooked grains are so much easier to pick up with chopsticks. Although easy-cook or "converted" rice is widely available, and will give the requisite fluffy, non-sticky texture, purists do not recommend it, as they believe it does not taste as good.

Steamed Rice

If you do not own a steamer, you may like to consider buying one of the pretty bamboo basket steamers that are on sale at Chinese food stores. They are not very expensive, and you can even serve the food in them.

I cup medium grain rice
I teaspoon salt

bring a large pan of salted water to the boil. Scatter in the rice, cover, and cook on a low heat for 5 minutes. Drain, run through with hot water, and drain again.

transfer the rice to a bamboo steamer or a vegetable steamer.

set the steamer over boiling water, taking care that the water does not bubble up through the rice.

use the handle of a wooden spoon to make several holes through the rice for the steam to circulate.

cover the pan and steam the rice for 45 minutes.

turn the rice on to a wide, flat platter and leave in a warm place for about 5 minutes to dry.

fluff it with a fork twice during that time to separate the grains and ensure even drying.

Serves 4
Preparation time: *5 minutes*
Cooking time: *50 minutes*

Meats

Pork Spareribs
with spicy chili sauce

Tender, succulent spareribs have always been prized by Chinese cooks. Cook them in this sizzling, spicy sauce for a mouth-watering treat.

Chili sauce

4 tablespoons clear honey

4 tablespoons wine vinegar

2 tablespoons light soy sauce

2 tablespoons Chinese wine or dry sherry

1 x 5-ounce can (⅔ cup) tomato paste

1 teaspoon chili powder

2 garlic cloves, crushed

2 pounds lean pork spareribs, cut into 2-inch pieces

2 tablespoons sunflower oil

2 dried red chilies, deseeded and cut into small rings

1 x 1-inch piece fresh root ginger, peeled and finely chopped

1 garlic clove, thinly sliced

1 dried red chili, deseeded and cut into small rings, to garnish (optional)

salt

make the chili sauce: mix all the ingredients together and set aside.

sprinkle the spareribs with salt.

heat the oil in a wok and quickly fry the red chilies to flavor it.

remove the chilies with a slotted spoon and discard them. Next, add the chopped ginger and garlic to the wok and stir-fry over moderate heat for 30 seconds.

add the spareribs and stir-fry for 5 minutes, until golden brown. Reduce the heat and cook gently for 10 minutes.

add the sauce to the wok, cover, and simmer gently for 25–30 minutes. Serve hot, garnished with the chili rings, if liked.

Serves 4–6
Preparation time: *15 minutes*
Cooking time: *40–45 minutes*

clipboard: Provide several small bowls of warm water and plenty of paper napkins whenever you are serving spareribs or other food that is usually eaten with the fingers.

Twice-Cooked Pork *with hot bean sauce*

12 ounces pork belly in one piece
½ cup bamboo shoots
2 celery stalks
2 green onions (scallions)
1 garlic clove
3 tablespoons sunflower oil
2 tablespoons Chinese wine or dry sherry
1 tablespoon light soy sauce
1 tablespoon chili bean paste

place the whole piece of pork in a pan of boiling water and cook for 25–30 minutes. Remove and leave to cool.

slice the meat thinly, cutting across the grain, into pieces not much larger than a postage stamp.

cut the bamboo shoots and celery into 2-inch chunks. Chop the green onions (scallions) and mince the garlic.

heat the oil in a wok or deep skillet until smoking.

add the green onions (scallions) and garlic to flavor the oil, then add the vegetables and stir-fry briefly.

add the pork, then the wine or sherry, soy sauce, and chili bean paste. Stir-fry for 2 minutes.

transfer to a warmed dish and serve immediately with noodles.

Serves 3–4
Preparation time: *15 minutes*
Cooking time: *35–40 minutes*

clipboard: This recipe combines two cooking methods in a technique known as "cross-cooking". It involves boiling and then stir-frying, to ensure full flavor and a crisp texture.

Stir-fried Pork and Eggplant

6 ounces boned lean pork, shredded

2 green onions (scallions), finely chopped

I slice of fresh root ginger, peeled and minced

I garlic clove, peeled and minced

I tablespoon soy sauce

I teaspoon Chinese wine or or dry sherry

1½ teaspoons cornstarch

2½ cups vegetable oil for deep-frying

I large or 2 small eggplant, cut into diamond-shaped chunks

I tablespoon chili sauce

3–4 tablespoons Chicken Broth (see page 11) or water

chopped green onion (scallion), to garnish

put the pork in a bowl with the green onions (scallions), ginger, garlic, soy sauce, wine or sherry, and cornstarch.

mix well, then leave to marinate for about 20 minutes.

heat the oil in a wok or deep-fat fryer to 350°F or until a cube of day-old bread browns in 45 seconds.

lower the heat, add the eggplant, and deep-fry for about 1½ minutes.

remove from the pan with a slotted spoon and drain.

pour off all but 1 tablespoon of oil from the pan, then add the pork, and stir-fry for about 1 minute.

add the eggplant and chili sauce, and cook for about 1½ minutes, then moisten with the broth or water.

simmer until the liquid has almost completely evaporated. Serve hot, with plain boiled rice, garnished with chopped green onions (scallions).

Serves 3–4
Preparation time: *10 minutes, plus 20 minutes marinating*
Cooking time: *10–15 minutes*

Cantonese Pork
in sweet-and-sour sauce

The extremes of sweet and sour in this sauce are meant to represent Yin and Yang in perfect harmony.

I pound pork fillet, cut into I-inch cubes
I teaspoon salt
pinch of pepper
½ teaspoon five-spice powder
2 tablespoons Chinese wine or dry sherry
I egg
3 tablespoons cornstarch
vegetable oil for deep-frying
2 tablespoons oil
I garlic clove, crushed
I onion, roughly chopped
I–2 green peppers, cored, deseeded and diced
I x 8-ounce can pineapple chunks, with juice
3 tablespoons wine vinegar
2 tablespoons sugar
4 tablespoons tomato ketchup

fill the saucepan with water and bring to the boil. Add the pork and boil until it changes color.

drain the pork, cool, and pat dry with absorbent paper towels.

mix together the salt, pepper, five-spice powder, wine or sherry, egg, and cornstarch. Add the pork and turn to coat well.

heat the oil to 350°F or until a cube of day-old bread browns in 45 seconds. Deep-fry the pork until brown. Drain thoroughly on absorbent paper towels.

heat the 2 tablespoons of oil in a skillet. Add the garlic and fry until brown. Add the onion and green bell pepper, and stir-fry for 1 minute. Stir in the pineapple juice with the vinegar, sugar, and tomato ketchup.

cook, stirring, until thickened. Add the pineapple and stir until heated through. Serve hot, garnished with the pineapple chunks.

Serves 4–6
Preparation time: *10 minutes*
Cooking time: *20–30 minutes*

clipboard: Five-spice powder is a Chinese mixture of five spices — anise pepper, star anise, cinnamon, cloves, and fennel seeds. It is strong and pungent and should be used sparingly.

Pork Slices
in honey and ginger sauce

Soaked and glazed in a luscious aromatic marinade, then quickly roasted, an economical cut of pork is cooked to perfection.

Marinade

2 tablespoons soy sauce

2 tablespoons Chinese wine or dry sherry

2 teaspoons sesame seed oil

I teaspoon salt

2 teaspoons ginger juice (see page 24)

2 tablespoons clear honey or dark corn syrup

2 tablespoons sugar

I–2 garlic cloves, crushed

3 pounds pork shoulder, cut into 2 x 2 x 8-inch pieces

mix together the marinade ingredients in a large dish.

add the pork and leave to marinate for at least 6 hours in the refrigerator, turning the meat occasionally.

place the pieces of pork on a wire rack in a roasting pan. Roast in a preheated moderate oven at 350°F for 40–45 minutes or until tender, basting with the pan juices frequently.

cut into serving pieces and arrange on a plate. Serve hot or cold.

Serves 6
Preparation time: *10 minutes, plus 6 hours marinating*
Cooking time: *40–45 minutes*
Oven temperature: *350°F*

clipboard: Pork shoulder is a good quality economical cut with an excellent flavor. Ask your butcher to chop it into evenly-sized pieces as specified in the ingredients, as this is difficult to do at home.

Fried Pork
with baby corn and snow peas

The luscious combination of flavors and textures in this quickly cooked dish is typical of Chinese cooking at its simplest and best.

1 tablespoon Chinese wine or dry sherry
1 tablespoon light soy sauce
1½ teaspoons cornstarch
1 pound pork fillet, sliced as thinly as possible
1 tablespoon sunflower oil
2 cups baby corn
1 teaspoon salt
¼ cup snow peas
1 x 15 ounce can straw mushrooms, drained
2 teaspoons sugar
2 teaspoons water

mix the wine or sherry and soy sauce with 1 teaspoon of the cornstarch. Add the pork and toss to coat well.

heat the oil in a wok or skillet and stir-fry the pork until it is lightly browned.

add the baby corn and salt, and stir-fry for 30 seconds. Add the snow peas and mushrooms, and stir-fry for 1 minute.

sprinkle in the sugar.

mix the remaining cornstarch with the water to make a thin paste and add this to the wok, stirring until the sauce is thickened.

transfer to a warmed serving platter and serve hot.

Serves 4
Preparation time: *5 minutes*
Cooking time: *5–8 minutes*

clipboard: Baby corn are usually available all year round at supermarkets. They are also sold in cans. If you use the canned variety, they need half the cooking time of fresh corn.

Red-cooked Pork
with sweet chestnuts

3–4 pounds pork belly
1½ teaspoons sugar
½ cup water
5½ tablespoons soy sauce
1 cup sweet chestnuts
5 tablespoons Chinese wine or dry sherry

cut the pork through the skin, lean, and fat, into 1½-inch pieces. Combine the sugar, water, and 4½ tablespoons of the soy sauce.

put the pork pieces in a flameproof casserole or Dutch oven and pour over just enough boiling water to cover.

simmer for 15 minutes, then drain off all the water. Pour in the soy sauce mixture. Stir the pork pieces in the sauce until well coated.

transfer to a preheated cool oven at 300°F and cook for 1 hour, stirring twice.

meanwhile, cook the chestnuts in boiling water for 30 minutes. Drain, then remove the shells and skin.

add the chestnuts to the pork with the wine or sherry and the remaining soy sauce. Stir well and return to the oven for a further 1 hour.

serve hot, on cooked shredded cabbage, if liked.

Serves 10
Preparation time: *20 minutes*
Cooking time: *2¼–3 hours*
Oven temperature: *300°F*

clipboard: Red-cooking is a unique Chinese style of cooking. The food is stewed in a mixture of soy sauce, water, and sugar, with wine and flavorings. It takes on an "auspicious" red color during cooking.

Braised Pork
with pumpkin and ginger

12 ounces lean pork
4 tablespoons soy sauce
3 tablespoons dry sherry
1 pound (2 cups) pumpkin flesh
4 green onions (scallions)
2 tablespoons oil
1 x 1-inch piece root ginger, shredded
2 garlic cloves, sliced

To garnish
carrot flowers
sliced green onion (scallion)
coriander (cilantro) leaves

cut the pork into ½-inch slices. Put the soy sauce and sherry in a bowl and add the pork.

mix well and leave to marinate for 20 minutes.

cut the pumpkin flesh into 1-inch cubes.

slice each green onion (scallion) into 3 pieces. Heat the oil in a wok or skillet, add the pumpkin, and fry quickly until browned.

add the green onions (scallions), ginger, and garlic, and cook for 1 minute.

add the pork and marinade and cook for 12–15 minutes, until the pork and pumpkin are tender.

spoon the mixture onto a warmed serving dish, garnish with carrot flowers, green onion (scallion) slices, and coriander (cilantro) leaves.

Serves 4–6
Preparation time: *15 minutes, plus 20 minutes marinating*
Cooking time: *about 20 minutes*

clipboard: To make carrot flowers, peel a whole carrot and trim the top and bottom. Cut out 6 "V"– shaped strips lengthwise down the sides of the carrot. Slice the carrot across into narrow rings, which will look just like little flowers.

Braised Lamb
with soy and mandarin sauce

4 mandarin oranges or 2 large navel oranges
1 tablespoon oil
4 leg-of-lamb steaks
6 green onions (scallions), shredded
1 tablespoon Chinese wine or sherry
1 tablespoon light soy sauce
⅔ cup Chicken Broth (see page 11)
1 tablespoon brown sugar
salt (optional)
freshly ground black pepper

pare the rind from the oranges thinly with a potato peeler. Squeeze the juice from the oranges and reserve.

shred the rind finely, blanch in boiling water for 5 minutes, and drain.

heat the oil in the wok. Add the lamb and fry until browned on both sides. Remove from the wok.

add the onions to the wok and fry for 3 minutes. Place the lamb on top of the onions.

add the juice squeezed from the oranges, orange rind shreds, the wine or sherry, soy sauce, chicken broth, brown sugar, and pepper.

cover with the lid and braise over a low heat for 40 minutes or until the lamb is tender.

check the seasoning during cooking, and add salt to taste if necessary.

serve on a bed of plain boiled rice, topped with the orange rind shreds.

Serves 4
Preparation time: *15 minutes*
Cooking time: *55 minutes*

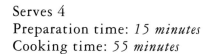

clipboard: Salt may be added to this recipe if liked — however remember that the soy sauce is salty, and you should always check the taste first before adding any salt.

Tung-Po Lamb
stir-fry with mixed vegetables

This is a light variation of a regional dish named after Tung Po, the famous Tang dynasty poet.

2 tablespoons sunflower oil
1½ pounds very lean lamb, thinly sliced
1 cup carrots, sliced diagonally
4 celery stalks, sliced diagonally
3 tablespoons light soy sauce
4 tablespoons Chinese wine or dry sherry
2 leeks, sliced
4 garlic cloves, thinly sliced
4 green onions (scallions), cut into 1-inch lengths
2-inch piece fresh root ginger, peeled and shredded
1 teaspoon lightly crushed black peppercorns
2 teaspoons brown sugar
flat-leaved parsley, to garnish

heat the oil in a wok or deep skillet, add the lamb, and cook until it is brown on all sides.

reduce the heat, add the carrots and celery, and stir-fry for 2 minutes.

stir in the soy sauce and wine or sherry. Cover and cook for 15 minutes, until the vegetables are tender.

add the leeks, garlic, green onions (scallions), and ginger and cook for 1 minute.

add the peppercorns and sugar, and heat through, stirring, until the sugar dissolves. Garnish with flat-leaved parsley and serve at once.

Serves 4–6
Preparation time: *15 minutes*
Cooking time: *20–25 minutes*

clipboard: The ideal cut of lamb for stir-frying is lamb fillet, the strip of tender boneless meat from the neck. If this is unavailable, use lean, fillet end of leg of lamb, from which all the fat has been removed.

Shredded Lamb

stir-fried with noodles and green onions

1 egg, beaten

1 tablespoon cornstarch

1½ tablespoons water

8 ounces lean lamb, shredded

3 tablespoons sunflower oil

2 tablespoons soy sauce

4–5 green onions (scallions), cut into 2-inch pieces

1¼ cups Chicken Broth (see page 11)

4 ounces cellophane noodles, soaked in hot water for 5 minutes and drained

1 tablespoon sesame seed oil

2 tablespoons Chinese wine or dry sherry

beat the egg with the cornstarch and water.

add the lamb and roll it in the mixture to coat it.

heat the oil in a skillet over high heat.

add the lamb and stir-fry for 1 minute. Sprinkle with the soy sauce and green onions (scallions), and stir-fry for 1 minute.

add the broth and noodles and bring to the boil, stirring. Simmer gently for 5 minutes.

sprinkle with the sesame seed oil and wine or sherry. Simmer for a further 1 minute. Serve hot on a bed of cellophane noodles.

Serves 4
Preparation time: *5 minutes*
Cooking time: *8–10 minutes*

clipboard: The technique of shredding food is often used in stir-frying, so it is useful to learn it. The simplest method is to stack thin slices of food on top of each other. Then, using a cleaver or a sharp knife, cut the food crosswise into thin, even strips.

Spring Lamb
stir-fried with garlic and sesame oil

12 ounces lamb fillet
2 tablespoons Chinese wine or dry sherry
2 tablespoons light soy sauce
1 tablespoon dark soy sauce
1 teaspoon sesame oil
2 tablespoons oil
6 garlic cloves, thinly sliced
1-inch piece root ginger, chopped
1 leek, thinly sliced diagonally
4 green onions (scallions), chopped

cut the lamb into thin slices across the grain.

make the marinade next: combine the wine or sherry with the soy sauces and sesame oil.

add the lamb and toss to coat. Leave to marinate for 15 minutes.

drain the lamb, reserving the marinade.

heat the oil in a wok or deep skillet, add the meat, and about 2 teaspoons of the marinade and fry briskly for about 2 minutes until the meat is well browned.

add the garlic, ginger, leek, and green onions (scallions) and fry for a further 3 minutes. Serve at once.

Serves 4
Preparation time: *5 minutes, plus 15 minutes marinating*
Cooking time: *5–7 minutes*

clipboard: Meat is thinly sliced before stir-frying to speed up cooking, and retain maximum tenderness. It should be cut across the grain using a sharp knife or cleaver. If you place the meat in the freezer to harden for about 1 hour before slicing, it will be easy to slice the meat wafer-thin, and it will have defrosted before cooking.

Stir-fried Beef

with white sesame seeds and baby mushrooms

12 ounces round steak
1 tablespoon light soy sauce
1 tablespoon dark soy sauce
1 tablespoon soft brown sugar
1 teaspoon sesame oil
1 tablespoon Chinese wine or dry sherry
2 tablespoons white sesame seeds
2 tablespoons sunflower oil
1 garlic clove, thinly sliced
2 carrots, sliced diagonally
2 celery stalks, sliced diagonally
½ cup button mushrooms, sliced

cut the steak into thin slices, slicing across the grain.

combine the soy sauces, sugar, sesame oil, and wine or sherry. Toss the meat in this mixture and leave to marinate for 15 minutes.

fry the sesame seeds in a dry skillet until they are golden.

heat the oil in a wok or skillet, add the garlic, celery, and carrots, and stir-fry briskly for 1 minute.

remove from the wok. Increase the heat, add the beef, and stir-fry for about 3 minutes until well browned.

return the vegetables to the wok, add the mushrooms, and cook for a further 30 seconds. Sprinkle with the toasted sesame seeds and serve.

Serves 4
Preparation time: *5 minutes, plus 15 minutes marinating*
Cooking time: *6–7 minutes*

clipboard: Sesame seeds are very popular in Chinese cooking because of their nutty flavor and excellent nutritional value. Black and white varieties are available, and they have the same flavor. The white variety are used here to contrast with the color of the beef.

Stir-fried Beef

in a hot chili sauce with garlic and ginger

Sizzling hot and full of flavor, this classic stir-fried beef dish will delight lovers of hot, spicy food.

1 pound round steak
2 tablespoons sunflower oil
2 dried red chilies
2 garlic cloves, sliced
1-inch piece fresh root ginger, shredded
4 green onions (scallions), shredded
2 tablespoons dark soy sauce
2 tablespoons light soy sauce
2 tablespoons Chinese wine or dry sherry
2 fresh green chilies, deseeded and chopped
salt

cut the steak into thin slices across the grain, and season well with salt.

heat the oil in a wok or deep skillet over a moderate heat and fry the red chilies for 1 minute to flavor the oil.

remove from the wok with a slotted spoon and discard.

increase the heat, then add the pieces of steak and stir-fry for 1 minute, until they are browned.

add the garlic, ginger, and green onions (scallions), and cook for 30 seconds.

pour this over the soy sauces and wine or sherry, add the chopped green chilies, and cook for a further minute.

transfer to a warmed serving dish and serve at once.

Serves 4
Preparation time: *20 minutes*
Cooking time: *4–5 minutes*

Spiced Beef
stir-fried with leeks and celery

*The addition of fresh, crunchy vegetables
to this aromatic stir-fry provides a
satisfying contrast of textures.*

1 pound round or sirloin steak
2 medium leeks
3 celery stalks
6 tablespoon oil
1 garlic clove, crushed with a pinch of salt
1 teaspoon red wine vinegar
1 teaspoon soy sauce
1 tablespoon sesame oil
1 tablespoon hot soy bean paste

cut the beef into small, thin slivers. Cut the leeks and celery into matchstick pieces.

heat 3 tablespoons oil in a wok or large skillet over a high heat.

add the leeks and celery. Stir-fry for 1 minute and remove.

add the remaining oil to the skillet. Add the steak and stir-fry until it has browned and all the moisture in the pan has evaporated.

stir in the garlic, vinegar, soy sauce, sesame oil, and soy bean paste.

add the vegetables and stir-fry for 1 minute.

transfer to a warmed serving dish and serve at once.

Serves 4–6
Preparation time: *10 minutes*
Cooking time: *10 minutes*

Shredded Beef
stir-fried in a hot Szechuan sauce

1 pound round or frying steak

2 tablespoons cornstarch

3 tablespoons sunflower oil

4 green onions (scallions), chopped

2 celery stalks, sliced diagonally

4 carrots, sliced diagonally

2 tablespoons light soy sauce

1 tablespoon hoisin sauce

3 teaspoons chili sauce

2 tablespoons Chinese wine or dry sherry

salt

cut the steak across the grain into long, thin slices.

toss the steak in the cornstarch and season with salt to taste.

heat the oil in a wok or skillet over a moderate heat. Add the green onions (scallions) and stir-fry for 1 minute.

add the sliced steak and cook for 4 minutes, stirring, until the meat is lightly browned.

add the celery and carrots and cook for 2 minutes. Stir in the soy, hoisin and chili sauces, and the wine or sherry.

bring to the boil and cook for 1 minute.

arrange on a warmed serving dish and serve at once.

Serves 4–6
Preparation time: *10–15 minutes*
Cooking time: *about 10 minutes*

clipboard: Hoisin sauce is a thick, brownish-red, soy-based sauce, much used in China both as a condiment and in cooked dishes. It is available in Chinese food stores and major supermarkets.

Steamed Beef

with peppers and bok choy

1 pound lean chuck steak

2 tablespoons dried Chinese mushrooms

⅔ cup boiling Chicken Broth (see page 11)

1 red bell pepper, cored, deseeded and cut into 1-inch strips

1 green bell pepper, cored, deseeded and cut into 1-inch strips

1 medium onion, thinly sliced

1 garlic clove, finely chopped

1 teaspoon cornstarch

3 tablespoons soy sauce

2 tablespoons sesame oil

1 teaspoon ground ginger

4–6 bok choy leaves

cut the beef into small, thin slices. Put the mushrooms into a bowl, pour on the broth, and leave to soak for 20 minutes.

drain the mushrooms and reserve the broth.

combine the beef, peppers, mushrooms, onion, and garlic in a bowl.

mix together the mushroom broth, cornstarch, soy sauce, oil, and ground ginger, and add to the beef.

line the top of a bamboo steamer with the bok choy leaves. Put in the beef mixture. Cover.

bring a small amount of water to the boil in a saucepan. Add a trivet or stand to the saucepan and set the steamer on top of it.

cover and steam for 1 hour 15 minutes or until the beef is quite tender. Serve straight from the steamer.

Serves 4–6
Preparation time: *20 minutes, plus 20 minutes soaking*
Cooking time: *1¼–1½ hours*

Stir-fried Beef

with Chinese plum sauce and mushrooms

Plums add a fragrant, fruity sweetness to this mouth-watering beef dish, as well as a succulent contrast of texture.

1 tablespoon sunflower oil
1 onion, thinly sliced
1 garlic clove, crushed
12 ounces lean beef, cut into thin slivers
2–3 dessert plums, pitted and sliced
3 flat mushrooms, sliced
1 tablespoon Chinese wine or dry sherry
2 teaspoons soft brown sugar
1 tablespoon dark soy sauce
2 teaspoons cornstarch
2 tablespoons water
2 chopped green onions (scallions)
(green part only), to garnish

heat the oil in a large skillet, add the onion, and fry for 2 minutes. Stir in the garlic and beef and stir-fry over a high heat for 2 minutes.

reduce the heat and add the plums and mushrooms. Continue to stir-fry for 1 minute, then stir in the wine or sherry, sugar, and soy sauce.

blend the cornstarch with the water to make a thin paste and add this mixture to the pan, stirring until the sauce has thickened.

transfer to a warmed dish and serve at once, garnished with chopped green onion (scallion).

Serves 4
Preparation time: *6 minutes*
Cooking time: *8 minutes*

Stir-fried Kidneys

with green onions and cauliflower flowerets

4 lambs' kidneys, halved and cored

2 tablespoons Chinese wine or sherry

1 small cauliflower, broken into flowerets

2 tablespoons oil

4 green onions (scallions), cut into 1-inch pieces

1 tablespoon cornstarch

1 tablespoon soy sauce

2 tablespoons water

1 teaspoon brown sugar

salt

score the kidney halves with shallow criss-cross cuts, about ½ inch apart. Marinate in the sherry for 10 minutes.

drain, reserving the marinade. Cook the cauliflower in boiling, salted water for 3 minutes. Drain thoroughly.

heat the oil in a skillet. Add the kidneys, green onions (scallions), and cauliflower, and fry for 2 minutes.

mix the cornstarch with the soy sauce, water, sugar, reserved marinade, and 1 teaspoon salt.

add to the pan and cook gently for 3 minutes, stirring until the sauce is thickened. Serve hot.

Serves 4
Preparation time: *5 minutes, plus
10 minutes marinating*
Cooking time: *8–10 minutes*

clipboard: Remove any membrane from the kidneys before removing the core. The kidney is scored with criss-cross cuts in order to ensure that maximum tenderness is maintained with speed of cooking.

Stir-fried Liver
with spinach and ginger

The pungent, earthy flavor of spinach blends perfectly with liver in this robust, quickly prepared, stir-fry dish.

12 ounces lamb's liver, cut into thin triangular slices
2 tablespoons cornstarch
4 tablespoons sunflower oil
6 cups fresh spinach, washed and drained
1 teaspoon salt
2 thin slices fresh root ginger, peeled
1 tablespoon light soy sauce
1 tablespoon Chinese wine or dry sherry
green onion (scallion), shredded, to garnish

blanch the slices of liver in boiling water for a few seconds. Drain and coat with cornstarch.

heat 2 tablespoons of the oil in a wok or skillet. Add the spinach and salt and stir-fry for 2 minutes.

remove from the pan and arrange around the edge of a warmed serving dish. Keep hot.

wipe the wok clean with absorbent paper towels. Heat the remaining oil in the wok until very hot.

add the ginger, liver, soy sauce, and wine or sherry. Stir-fry briskly for 1–2 minutes — avoid overcooking or the liver will become tough.

pour the mixture over the spinach and garnish with green onions (scallions).

Serves 4
Preparation time: *10 minutes*
Cooking time: *4–5 minutes*

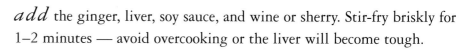

clipboard: Blanching liver in boiling water is a good way of ensuring that it remains tender during the cooking process.

Lion's Head Casserole *with garlic*

1½ pounds lean twice-ground pork,
1 teaspoon salt
2 garlic cloves, crushed
1 x 2-inch piece fresh root ginger,
peeled and chopped
4 tablespoons light soy sauce
3 tablespoons Chinese wine or dry sherry
4 green onions (scallions), chopped
1 tablespoon cornstarch
oil, for deep frying
1¼ cups Beef Broth (see page 10)
8 cups fresh spinach
green onion (scallions), chopped, to garnish
(optional)

mix the pork with the salt, garlic, ginger, and 1 tablespoon each of the soy sauce, and wine or sherry.

add half of the chopped green onions (scallions). Mix in the cornstarch and divide the mixture into balls the size of a walnut.

heat the oil in a wok or deep fryer to 325°F or until a cube of day-old bread browns in 45 seconds.

deep-fry the pork balls until golden. Drain well, then place in a clean pan with the remaining soy sauce, wine or sherry, and green onions (scallions).

spoon the broth over the meat, cover, and simmer for 15–20 minutes.

wash the spinach leaves and cook in the water clinging to the leaves. When tender, drain well and transfer to a warmed serving platter.

arrange the meatballs on top and garnish with chopped green onion (scallion), if liked. Serve at once.

Serves 4–6
Preparation time: *20 minutes*
Cooking time: *25–30 minutes*

clipboard: This traditional eastern Chinese dish is named for the alleged resemblance of the meatballs to a lion's head. The meatballs are usually served with noodles arranged on top to look like a lion's mane.

Mongolian Hotpot

8 ounces cellophane noodles, or
1 pound egg noodles
8 ounces lean boned pork, beef, or lamb, or
a mixture of all 3 meats, thinly sliced
8 ounces boneless chicken breast, skinned
and thinly sliced
1 cup shrimp (whole) or scallops (thinly sliced),
or a mixture of both
8 ounces fish fillets (sole, flounder, cod, haddock),
thinly sliced
2 cups button mushrooms
1 head Chinese (Napa) cabbage or romaine lettuce
1½ cups firm bean curd (tofu), cut in small pieces
7½ cups clear broth
1 teaspoon salt
2–3 tablespoons Chinese rice wine or dry sherry

Sauce
4 tablespoons light soy sauce
4 tablespoons dark soy sauce
1 tablespoon sugar
2 teaspoons sesame seed oil
3–4 green onions (scallions), finely shredded
3–4 slices fresh root ginger, peeled and finely
shredded
1–2 garlic cloves, peeled and crushed
1 tablespoon chili sauce (optional)

soak the noodles in boiling hot water until soft, rinse under cold running water, then drain. Arrange the meats, shellfish, fish, vegetables, and bean curd on separate plates or in bowls, then place them on the table.

mix all the ingredients for the sauce together, then divide equally between 4–6 saucers. Place them on the table at individual place settings.

place the hot pot in the center of the table. Light the charcoal in the funnel and fill the circular trough below with the broth.

add the salt and rice wine or sherry, a few Chinese (Napa) cabbage leaves or lettuce, mushrooms, noodles, and bean curd. Bring to the boil. Each diner picks up a few pieces of meat or fish and swirls them in the broth for a few seconds. When the slices begin to curl and turn color, they are removed from the liquid and dipped into the sauce, before eating.

more vegetables and noodles can be added to the pot from time to time, and eaten with the meat, fish and bean curd. When the meat and fish have been eaten, top up with more broth, add the remaining vegetables and noodles, and recharge with more charcoal if necessary.

bring to the boil and cook for about 1–2 minutes, then ladle the contents into individual bowls. Serve as a soup with the remaining dip sauce, to finish off the meal.

Serves 4–6
Preparation time: *15 minutes*
Cooking time: *about 10 minutes*

clipboard: Inexpensive hot pots or "fire kettles" can be bought at Chinese supermarkets. This is a great way of entertaining, especially in winter. Ensure the room is well ventilated to allow the charcoal fumes to escape and extinguish the charcoal when not in use.

Herbs and vegetables

Dried red chilies

Garlic

Shiitake mushroom

Water chestnut

Dried red chilies

Dried chilies are a relatively recent addition to Chinese cooking, though they are now used extensively, particularly in Szechuan dishes. Chilies are perfect for flavoring oil in stir-frying, and in spicy hot-flavored pastes. Stored correctly they will keep for ages and maintain their red color and fiery flavor. Use them with care, as they can be searingly hot.

Shiitake mushroom

The shiitake mushroom has a golden brown cap and light colored gills and stem. The stems can sometimes be tough and are often discarded, but the caps are intensely fragrant. In China they are often dried, making the flavor even more intense. They are one of the key ingredients in Chinese cooking.

Garlic

Garlic is a bulb-shaped, root vegetable, composed of a series of cloves wrapped in a white papery skin. Garlic has been used for thousands of years and has been a major ingredient in the history of cooking. The strong, pungent aroma and flavor add character to any savory dish. Garlic is used extensively in Chinese cooking.

Water chestnut

The water chestnut is similar in appearance to the chestnut. This white nut with a brown skin is technically the corm of a species of water grass. Water chestnuts have a crunchy texture and sweet taste even when cooked and are used extensively in Chinese dishes, both in cooked foods and in salads. Water chestnuts can be bought fresh or canned.

Bamboo shoot

The bamboo shoot is part of the bamboo plant which is found all over tropical Asia.

Bamboo shoot

Onion

Coriander (Cilantro)

Tofu

Green onions (scallions)

It is a pale ivory color, and the texture varies according to the season. The sweet, crunchy shoots have been used in Chinese cooking since the sixth century. The shoots are more frequently available canned than fresh.

Tofu

Tofu is a curd made from soya beans. It is highly nutritious, and is creamy white in color with a smooth texture and bland flavor. The curd is pressed and set into cakes. The Chinese use tofu in soups, salads, and stir-fry dishes. Dried tofu is used as a meat substitute in vegetarian dishes. Fresh tofu should be eaten on the day of purchase.

Onion

The Chinese use the brown-skinned white onion in many of their dishes because its powerful aroma and sharp taste adds great flavor to cooking. It is also used in pickled dishes.

Green onion (scallion)

The green onion, known as a scallion on the eastern seaboard of the United States, has a milder flavor than the fully-grown onion. It is particularly prized in Chinese cooking, as much for this delicate flavor as for its attractive shape and color. It is a very popular garnish, especially when the green ends are slit into tassels or curls.

Coriander (Cilantro)

Coriander, known as cilantro in the west of the United States, is sometimes called Chinese Parsley.

It has bright green, lacy leaves, white flowers, and an intense, characteristic aroma and flavor. The leaves, roots, and seeds are all used in Chinese cooking. Coriander is very popular in Chinese, Thai, and other oriental styles of cooking.

Vegetable
dishes

Bean Curd *and sesame salad with peanuts*

12½ cups bean curd (tofu)
4 ounces skinless roast chicken
½ long cucumber
2 tablespoons roasted peanuts
oil, for deep frying

Dressing
2 tablespoons sesame paste
1 tablespoon soy sauce
1 tablespoon white wine vinegar
1 tablespoon Chinese wine or dry sherry
1 teaspoon chili sauce
1 garlic clove, crushed with a pinch of salt
2 tablespoons cold water

cut the bean curd, chicken, and cucumber into ½-inch dice. Put the cucumber, chicken, and peanuts into a bowl.

make the dressing: put the sesame paste into a bowl and gradually work in the remaining ingredients to give the consistency of thick mayonnaise.

heat a deep pan of oil to 350°F or until a cube of day-old bread browns in 45 seconds. Add the cubes of bean curd and deep-fry until they are just turning color.

remove and drain. Heat the oil to 375°F. Return the cubes of bean curd to the pan, and deep-fry until crisp and golden.

drain the bean curd quickly and mix into the ingredients in the bowl. Mix in the dressing.

serve the salad immediately — if the bean curd is left too long, it will lose its crispness.

Serves 4
Preparation time: *45 minutes*
Cooking time: *8 minutes*

clipboard: Also known as tofu, bean curd is highly nutritious. After cooking the texture is like a honeycomb, so the peanuts add a contrast of crunchy texture. You can make this dish suitable for vegetarians if you like — simply leave out the chicken.

Crispy Bean Curd

with tomato sauce

oil, for deep-frying
6 pieces bean curd (tofu), halved
then cut into small triangles
3 large tomatoes, skinned, deseeded
and finely chopped
⅔ cup Chicken Broth (see page 11)
1 tablespoon *nam pla* (fish sauce)
pinch of salt
⅓ teaspoon sugar
2 green onion (scallion) tops, cut into fine strips

heat the oil in a wok or deep fat fryer, add the bean curd, and fry until it is golden brown. Remove from the oil with a slotted spoon and set aside.

place the tomatoes in a medium saucepan with the chicken broth, *nam pla*, salt, and sugar.

bring to the boil, reduce the heat and simmer for 15–20 minutes.

add the bean curd and simmer for a further 10–15 minutes. The sauce should be thick and tasty.

serve immediately, with strips of green onion (scallion) arranged on top.

Serves 4
Preparation time: *15 minutes*
Cooking time *40–45 minutes*

clipboard: The use of tomatoes is unusual in Oriental cookery. This recipe has been influenced by Vietnamese cuisine, which in turn is French influenced. Use a tomato variety that is grown for its flavor. Please note that this recipe uses chicken broth and *nam pla* (a fish sauce). To make a vegetarian alternative, use vegetable broth and a seaweed-based seasoning (available from health food stores).

Vegetables *in silken tofu and tahini dressing*

This is an elegant dish, made extra healthy and nutritious by the use of tofu in the dressing.

3 dried shiitake mushrooms
½ fennel bulb
2 slices cooked ham
1 small carrot, peeled
¼ cup green beans, trimmed
1¾ cups Chicken Broth (see page 11)
1 tablespoon light soy sauce
2 teaspoons sugar

Dressing
½ cup silken tofu (bean curd)
2 tablespoons tahini
2½ tablespoons sugar
1 teaspoon salt

soak the mushrooms in boiling water for 20 minutes. Drain, discard the hard stalks, and cut the caps into strips.

cut the fennel, ham, carrot, and green beans into diagonal strips.

bring the broth to the boil in a pan with the soy sauce and sugar. Add the vegetables and simmer for 10 minutes. Allow to cool.

make the dressing: drop the tofu into a pan of boiling water, bring back to the boil, then drain.

place on a board, top with a plate, and weight to squeeze out excess moisture. Force the tofu through a sieve into a bowl.

add the tahini, sugar, and salt. Mix well.

drain the vegetables, reserving the liquid, and add them to the dressing with the ham. Add a little broth to thin if necessary. Serve cold.

Serves 4
Preparation time: *20–30 minutes*
Cooking time: *15–20 minutes*

clipboard: Please note that this recipe uses meat and chicken broth. To make a vegetarian alternative, use vegetable broth and omit the ham.

Braised Chinese Vegetables

2–3 tablespoons dried wood ears (cloud ears) or
5–6 dried shiitake mushrooms
I cup firm bean curd (tofu)
salt
4 tablespoons vegetable oil
½ cup carrots, peeled and sliced
½ cup snow peas, trimmed
I cup shredded Chinese (Napa) cabbage
½ cup canned, sliced bamboo shoots or
whole baby sweetcorn
I teaspoon sugar
I tablespoon light soy sauce
I teaspoon cornstarch
I tablespoon water
I teaspoon sesame seed oil, to finish (optional)

soak the wood ears or Chinese dried mushrooms in water to cover for 20–25 minutes; discard the hard roots, then rinse. Cut the mushrooms into small slices.

cut each cake of bean curd into about 12 small pieces, then put them in a saucepan of lightly salted, boiling water for 2–3 minutes, so that they become firm. Remove with a perforated spoon and drain.

heat about half of the oil in a flameproof casserole or heavy-based saucepan until hot. Add the pieces of bean curd and fry until lightly browned on both sides. Remove the bean curd, then heat the remaining oil in the pan.

add the vegetables and stir-fry for about 1–2 minutes. Return the bean curd to the pan, add 1 teaspoon salt, the sugar, and soy sauce and stir well. Cover, reduce the heat, and braise for 2–3 minutes.

mix the cornstarch to a smooth paste with the water. Pour the paste over the vegetables and stir. Increase the heat to high to thicken the sauce, then sprinkle in the sesame seed oil (if using).

Serves 4
Preparation time: *15 minutes, plus 20–25 minutes soaking*
Cooking time: *8–10 minutes*

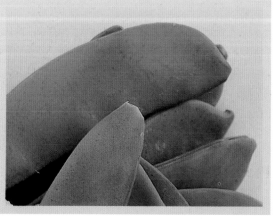

clipboard: Wood ears, also known as cloud ears, are dried black Chinese fungi with a delicate flavor. They are available from Chinese grocery stores. Soak them in warm water before use.

Chinese Cabbage
braised with mushrooms

I medium Chinese (Napa) cabbage

I½ cups canned straw mushrooms, drained, or I cup fresh button mushrooms

4 tablespoons sunflower oil

2 teaspoons salt

I teaspoon sugar

I tablespoon cornstarch

3 tablespoons water

¼ cup milk

separate and wash the leaves and cut each one in half lengthwise. If using fresh mushrooms, wipe the caps (do not peel), and trim the stalks.

heat 2 tablespoons of the oil in a wok over moderate heat. Add the Chinese (Napa) cabbage and stir-fry for 1 minute.

add 1½ teaspoons of the salt with the sugar and stir-fry for 1 minute. Remove the cabbage and arrange neatly on a warmed serving platter. Keep it hot.

mix the cornstarch to a smooth paste with the water. Heat the remaining oil in the wok until it is hot, add the mushrooms and remaining salt, and stir-fry for 1 minute.

add the cornstarch paste and the milk and stir constantly until the sauce is smooth, white, and thickened.

pour the sauce evenly over the cabbage and serve at once.

Serves 4
Preparation time: *20 minutes*
Cooking time: *5–10 minutes*

clipboard: Vary this dish by using different mushrooms. Chinese dried mushrooms should be soaked first before using, or, for another really interesting flavor, use shiitake mushrooms.

Festive New Year Pickle

with cucumber, nuts, cauliflower, and cabbage

5 cabbage leaves
1 cucumber
3 carrots, trimmed
1 head cauliflower
1½ quarts vinegar
20 shallots, chopped
2 tablespoons root ginger, shredded
1 thumb-size piece fresh turmeric
3 red chilies, deseeded and chopped
2 teaspoons shrimp paste
5 macadamia nuts
1 large onion, chopped
6 tablespoons sunflower oil
2 cups peanuts
3 tablespoons sugar
4 tablespoons sesame seeds

cut the cabbage, cucumber, and carrots into narrow strips. Separate the cauliflower into flowerets.

bring the vinegar to the boil in a saucepan and drop in handfuls of the cabbage, cucumber, carrots, cauliflower, and shallots to scald for 1 minute. Lift out and drain well.

work the ginger, turmeric, chilies, shrimp paste, macadamia nuts, and onion to a thick paste.

heat the oil in a wok or skillet and fry this mixture for 5 minutes. Place in a glass or enamel (not metal) bowl and mix in the vegetables thoroughly. Refrigerate for at least 1 day, preferably longer.

to serve, mix in the peanuts and sugar and sprinkle the sesame seeds over the pickle.

Serves 4
Preparation time: *45 minutes, plus a day chilling*
Cooking time: *8–10 minutes*

clipboard: The Chinese adore pickles, and this spicy example (called Achar) is prepared in great quantities to celebrate the Chinese New Year.

Crispy Vegetables

deep-fried and served with a spicy avocado dip

Dip

1–2 garlic cloves, chopped
4 tomatoes, peeled, deseeded and chopped
1 teaspoon chili powder
2 avocados, peeled and pitted
1 tablespoon coriander (cilantro), freshly chopped
pinch of ground coriander (cilantro) (optional)

Batter

1 cup all-purpose flour
pinch of salt
1 tablespoon sunflower oil
⅔ cup water
2 egg whites, stiffly beaten

Stir-fry

sunflower oil for deep-frying
2 cups mixed vegetables, such as cauliflower or broccoli flowerets, green beans, whole mushrooms, snow peas, and strips of zucchini

make the dip: place all the ingredients in a blender and blend to a smooth purée. Spoon into a serving dish and chill.

make the batter: sift the flour and salt into a bowl. Gradually beat in the oil and water, then fold in the egg whites.

heat the oil in a wok or frying pan to 350°F, or until a cube of day-old bread browns in 45 seconds.

dip the vegetables in the batter, then deep-fry them in batches for 2–3 minutes, until they are crisp and golden.

make sure the oil comes back to full heat after each batch.

drain the vegetables on absorbent paper towels and serve with the dip.

Serves 6
Preparation time: *15 minutes*
Cooking time: *25–30 minutes*

Spicy Long Beans
with Chinese fish cake

This is a deliciously spicy Chinese recipe for fresh runner beans. Long beans are traditionally used as they are meant to symbolize and ensure a long, happy, life.

8 long or 16 short green beans

1 block Chinese fish cake (see clipboard)

3 tablespoons sunflower oil

2 garlic cloves, crushed

1 tablespoon chili bean paste

⅔ cup water

1 teaspoon salt

cut the beans into 2-inch lengths, wash, and drain.

slice the fish cake into lengths of a similar size.

heat the oil in a wok or skillet and fry the garlic until light brown.

add the chili bean paste and cook, stirring all the time, for 1 minute.

add the beans and cook, stirring well, for 2–3 minutes. Add the fish cake and water.

increase the heat and stir-fry briskly for 1–2 minutes. Add salt to taste and serve immediately.

Serves 4
Preparation time: *10 minutes*
Cooking time: *10–12 minutes*

clipboard: Fish cake is sold in blocks at Chinese supermarkets and can be sliced as required. It is an excellent way of adding flavor and protein to stir-fried vegetables.

Beansprouts and Green Beans
stir-fry with green onions

2 cups fresh beansprouts
I cup baby green beans
3–4 tablespoons sunflower oil
I green onion (scallion), finely chopped
I teaspoon salt
I teaspoon sugar
I teaspoon sesame oil

wash and rinse the beansprouts in a basin of cold water, discarding the husks and other particles that float to the surface.

drain well. Top, tail, and halve the green beans.

heat the oil in a wok until it is smoking. Add the green onion (scallion) to flavor the oil, then add the beans and stir a few times.

add the beansprouts and stir-fry for 30 seconds.

add the salt and sugar and stir-fry for 1 minute more.

serve hot, sprinkled with sesame oil.

Serves 4
Preparation time: *10 minutes*
Cooking time: *3–4 minutes*

clipboard: It is best to use fresh beansprouts for this dish, so you should buy them on the day you plan to use them. Canned beansprouts do not have the crunchy texture required for this recipe.

Mustard-pickled Eggplant

Pickles are very important in Chinese cooking, as they provide a piquant salty or sour contrast with the other foods that are served at a typical meal.

1 medium eggplant,
or 6 small long (Japanese) eggplants
3 cups water
1 tablespoon salt
cucumber rings, to garnish (optional)

Dressing
1 teaspoon mustard powder
3 tablespoons soy sauce
3 tablespoons Chinese wine or medium dry sherry
4 tablespoons sugar

cut the eggplant in ⅛-inch slices, and cut each slice into quarters. Soak in the water, with the salt added, for 1 hour.

make the dressing: put all the ingredients in a bowl and stir well.

drain the eggplant slices and pat dry with absorbent paper towels.

arrange them carefully in a glass or ceramic serving bowl and pour the dressing over evenly and slowly.

cover the bowl with plastic wrap and chill in the refrigerator for several hours or overnight before serving, to allow the flavors to marry.

garnish with the cucumber rings, if liked.

Serves 4
Preparation time: *15 minutes, plus 1 hour soaking and chilling overnight*

clipboard: To make cucumber rings, cut ¼-inch slices from an unpeeled cucumber and remove the seeds. Make a cut in one ring and loop it through another.

Bok Choy
in sweet-and-sour sauce

This recipe for bok choy makes an attractive and different-tasting dish. Children will often enjoy it even if they refuse to eat other kinds of cabbage!

3 tablespoons oil
I tablespoon butter
I bok choy, cored and shredded
I teaspoon salt

Sauce
I½ tablespoons cornstarch
5 tablespoons water
I½ tablespoons soy sauce
2½ tablespoons sugar
3½ tablespoons vinegar
3½ tablespoons orange juice
2½ tablespoons tomato paste
I½ tablespoons Chinese wine or sherry

heat the oil and butter in a skillet. Add the cabbage and sprinkle with the salt. Stir-fry for 2 minutes.

reduce the heat to low and simmer gently for 5–6 minutes.

mix the sauce ingredients in another pan.

bring to the boil and simmer for 4–5 minutes, stirring continuously, until the sauce thickens and becomes translucent.

transfer the cabbage to a serving dish and pour the sauce over it. Serve hot.

Serves 4
Preparation time: *5 minutes*
Cooking time: *11–13 minutes*

clipboard: Bok choy, also called pak choy, is widely available at greengrocers and supermarkets. It has a crisp, juicy texture, and mild mustard flavor. Mustard greens or Swiss chard (silverbeet) can be substituted.

Pickled Green Salad *with bok choy and cucumber*

This is a cool, refreshing, and delicately pretty pickled salad, which is much enjoyed in Chinese cooking as a contrast to hot, fiery dishes.

4 cucumbers, peeled
2 bok choy, cored and chopped
2 teaspoons salt
1 teaspoon garlic, crushed
1 teaspoon Szechuan or black peppercorns, ground
1 teaspoon sugar
1 tablespoon light soy sauce
2 tablespoons sesame oil
1 tablespoon red wine vinegar

crush the cucumber until cracks appear on the surface. Quarter it lengthwise, then cut into pieces.

put in a bowl with the bok choy, sprinkle with salt, and leave for 2 hours.

rinse the salt from the vegetables and drain on absorbent paper towels. Mix together the garlic, pepper, sugar, soy sauce, oil, and vinegar.

pour this over the vegetables, mix well, and allow to stand for at least 3 hours before serving.

Serves 4–6
Preparation time: *15 minutes, plus 3 hours standing*

clipboard: Szechuan peppercorns are not related to ordinary pepper. They are reddish-brown, and are far more aromatic and pungent than ordinary peppercorns. The cucumber in this recipe is salted in order to extract its indigestible juices and to ensure as crisp a texture as possible.

Fruits and vegetables

Bok choy (Pak choy)

Chinese (Napa) cabbage

Eggplant

Baby corn

Bok choy (Pak choy)

Bok choy is also known as pak choy. It is now widely available in supermarkets, as well as from Chinese food stores. Bok choy has thick white stems and dark green leaves. The flavor is mild and it can be eaten raw or braised. There is a smaller variety known as a baby bok choy. Braised whole, this is a popular vegetable dish served at festive occasions.

Chinese (Napa) cabbage

Chinese leaves are pale green leaves which grow tightly packed to form a long, slim, tapering cabbage. It has a clean, delicate flavor and can be used in salads, stir-fries or as a steamed vegetable. It is also frequently used in Chinese soups. Originating in Eastern Asia several hundred years ago, it is best eaten from early autumn to winter, but is now imported all year round.

Baby corn

Baby corn is a delicious, finger-sized corn cob which is pale yellow in color, with a delicate, sweet flavor; a miniature version of corn-on-the-cob. Baby corn is ideal as an ingredient in stir-fry dishes and can also be plain boiled as a separate vegetable accompaniment. It is widely available in the summer and fall months.

Eggplant

The eggplant is so-called because of its shape, though there is a wide variation in size, color, flavor, and shape. All eggplants have a smooth skin and pale green to cream-colored flesh. The eggplant is technically a fruit but is usually cooked and eaten as a vegetable. The eggplant can be steamed, boiled, broiled, or sautéed.

The baby eggplant is a miniature version, prized for its tender, sweet flesh. It is a very popular ingredient in

Lychees

Pineapple

Lemon

Plum

Chinese cooking, especially in traditional winter pickles. The long, thin, purple eggplant referred to as Japanese or Asian eggplant is also used in Chinese cooking.

Plum

The plum is a small oval-shaped fruit with a shiny skin, ranging in color from yellow to purple. It has sweet, juicy flesh with a single pit. It is delicious eaten by itself and is used in Chinese cooking for both savory and sweet dishes. A delicious plum sauce is often served with duck. Plums are at their best in summer and early fall.

Lychees

The lychee is a small, oval, cherry-sized fruit with an attractive pink or red outer casing which is covered with tiny bumps. The translucent white flesh encases a single pit. The lychee, the fruit of an evergreen tree from southeast China, has a subtle, grape-like flavor. Lychees are used in fruit salads or in savory dishes. They are at their best in summer, but are available canned all year round.

Pineapple

Pineapple is a tropical fruit with a thick yellow-brown skin and a crown of spiny leaves. The yellow flesh is sweet and juicy and is delicious eaten by itself or added to savory or sweet dishes. Peak season for pineapple is spring but it is also available canned. It is named because of its resemblance to a pine cone.

Lemon

The lemon is an oval citrus fruit with tart-tasting flesh. It is used as an addition to dishes rather than being eaten by itself. The acid juice and fragrant rind are used in sweet and savory dishes. The lemon probably originated in northern India. It is a good source of vitamin C and is easily available all year round.

Desserts

Candy Apples
Peking-style

These scrumptious apple pieces, encased in crisp, fine, taffy, make a popular dessert, served in Chinese restaurants all over the world.

1 cup all-purpose flour

1 egg

⅓ cup water, plus 2 tablespoons

4 crisp apples, peeled, cored and cut into thick slices

2½ cups sunflower oil, plus 1 tablespoon

6 tablespoons sugar

3 tablespoons dark corn syrup

mix together the flour, egg, and ⅓ cup of the water to make a batter. Dip each piece of apple into the batter.

heat 2½ cups of the oil in a wok or deep skillet to 350°F or until a cube of bread browns in 45 seconds.

deep-fry the apple pieces for 2 minutes, then remove and drain on absorbent paper towels.

heat together the sugar in another pan, and add the remaining oil and water. Dissolve the sugar over a gentle heat, then simmer for 5 minutes, stirring constantly.

add the corn syrup and boil until the hard crack stage is reached, at 304°F, or until it forms brittle threads when dropped into iced water. Add the fried apples and turn to coat each piece.

remove the apple pieces with a slotted spoon and drop into iced water.

Serves 4
Preparation time: *15 minutes*
Cooking time: *about 16 minutes*

Banana Fritters
deep-fried in batter

The addition of lime as a flavoring for this traditional Chinese dessert provides an unusual and refreshing touch.

1 cup self-rising flour
3 tablespoons rice flour
½ teaspoon salt
rind of 1 lime, finely grated (optional)
vegetable oil, for deep-frying
8 small bananas

To serve

12 limes, cut into quarters
superfine sugar, to taste

sift the flours and salt into a bowl. Add about 1 cup cold water, and whisk thoroughly to make a smooth, coating batter.

stir in the grated lime rind (if using).

heat the oil in a hot wok or deep-fat fryer. Meanwhile, peel the bananas, spear them one at a time with a skewer, and dip into the batter until they are evenly coated.

deep-fry the bananas in batches until they are crisp and golden. Remove with a perforated spoon. Drain on absorbent paper towels.

serve hot, with the lime wedges and sugar for sprinkling.

Serves 8
Preparation time: *15 minutes*
Cooking time: *12–16 minutes*

clipboard: If possible, buy very small bananas for these fritters. They look better than large ones and are usually sweeter in flavor. Small, red bananas look very attractive.

Fried Sweet Potato Balls

with candied fruits and sesame seeds

Created from sweet potatoes, an unusual dessert ingredient, these are absolutely delicious!

1 pound sweet potatoes (yams)
1 cup rice flour
2 tablespoons soft brown sugar
½ cup mixed candied fruits, chopped
4 tablespoons sesame seeds, lightly toasted
oil, for deep-frying

cook the potatoes in boiling water for 20 minutes until tender; drain and peel them.

mash the flesh and gradually beat in the flour and sugar. Stir in the candied fruits.

roll the mixture into walnut-sized balls with dampened hands, then coat with sesame seeds.

heat the oil in a wok or deep-fryer and deep-fry the potato balls for 5–7 minutes, until golden brown. Drain on absorbent paper towels. Serve hot.

Serves 4–6
Preparation time: *10 minutes*
Cooking time: *25–27 minutes*

clipboard: Sesame seeds are often toasted before using, in order to bring out their deliciously nutty flavor. To do this easily, simply dry-fry them in the wok for 2–3 minutes, or until they are golden brown.

Rice Fritters
with coconut and vanilla

These delectable tidbits simply melt in the mouth — they are crispy outside and softly succulent within.

⅔ cup medium grain rice, cooked (see page 132)
2 eggs, beaten
3 tablespoons sugar
½ teaspoon vanilla extract
½ cup all-purpose flour
1 tablespoon baking powder
pinch of salt
2 tablespoons shredded coconut
vegetable oil, for deep-frying
sifted powdered sugar, for sprinkling

put the rice, eggs, sugar, and vanilla in a bowl, and mix well.

sift together the flour, baking powder, and salt, then stir into the rice mixture. Stir in the coconut.

heat the oil in a deep fat fryer to 350°F or until a cube of day-old bread browns in 45 seconds.

drop tablespoonfuls of the mixture into the hot oil, one at a time, and deep-fry until golden on all sides. Drain on absorbent paper towels.

transfer to a warmed serving dish and sprinkle with a generous amount of powdered sugar. Serve hot.

Makes about 20
Preparation time: *10 minutes*
Cooking time: *about 8–10 minutes*

clipboard: As rice is such a staple food in China, it is not surprising that so many desserts are based on sweetened rice. Many of these are essential fare at the festive meals that punctuate the year.

Plum Blossom and Snow

The fruit symbolizes the first blossom of spring, and the white topping is the snow left over after winter.

6 dessert apples
6 bananas
2 lemons
6 eggs, separated
1½ cups sugar
9 tablespoons milk
9 tablespoons cornstarch
rind of 1 lime, thinly pared, to decorate

peel and core the apples and slice thinly. Peel the bananas and slice thinly. With a potato peeler, thinly pare the rind of 1 lemon and set aside for the decoration. Squeeze the juice from both lemons. Arrange the apple and banana in alternate layers in 12 individual ovenproof dishes, sprinkling each layer with a little of the lemon juice.

put the egg yolks in a heavy-based saucepan with the sugar, milk, cornstarch, and ½ cup plus 1 tablespoon cold water. Stir well to mix, then heat very gently, stirring all the time, until smooth.

pour the custard mixture over the fruit. Beat the egg whites until stiff, then spread over the top. Bake in a preheated hot oven at 425°F for 5 minutes, or until the top is crisp and golden. Remove the dishes from the oven and leave until completely cooled.

meanwhile, prepare the decoration. Plunge the pared lemon and lime rinds into a saucepan of boiling water and blanch for 2 minutes. Drain; rinse under cold running water, then pat dry with absorbent paper towels, and cut into thin strips. Sprinkle evenly over the top of the cold desserts just before serving.

Serves 12
Preparation time: *30 minutes*
Cooking time: *about 5 minutes*
Oven temperature: *425°F*

Almond Float
with mixed fruits

Cool and delicately flavored, this almond-scented float provides a light, clean-tasting finish to a meal.

1 tablespoon agar or vegetable gelatin, or 2 tablespoons powdered, unflavored gelatin

4 tablespoons sugar

1¼ cups milk

1 teaspoon almond extract

1 x 14-ounce can apricots, or mixed fruit salad

2 tablespoons white grapes, peeled and deseeded

dissolve the agar or gelatin in 1¼ cups water over a gentle heat. (If you are using unflavored gelatin, dissolve it in the water according to the package instructions.)

dissolve the sugar in 1¼ cups water in a separate saucepan, then combine with the dissolved setting agent, and add the milk and almond flavoring. Pour this mixture into a large serving bowl.

leave until cold, then chill in the refrigerator for at least 3 hours, until it is completely set.

to serve, cut into small cubes and place in a serving bowl. Add the canned fruit and syrup, then add the grapes, and mix well. Serve chilled.

Serves 4
Preparation time: *20 minutes, plus 3 hours setting*
Cooking time: *20 minutes*

clipboard: Agar is an extremely useful setting agent which has no flavor of its own, and does not require refrigeration.

Almond Cookies

These fragrant cookies are not a typical dessert, they are more of an end-of-meal snack to clear the palate. They are very popular with the family, so make plenty, and keep them in an airtight storage jar.

1½ cups all-purpose flour
pinch of salt
½ teaspoon baking soda
6 tablespoons lard
2 tablespoons ground almonds
3 tablespoons sugar
1 egg
½ teaspoon almond extract
15 blanched almonds
1 egg yolk, beaten with 1 tablespoon water

sift the flour with the salt and baking soda.

rub in the lard, mix in the ground almonds and sugar. Bind the mixture with the egg and almond extract and knead into a pliable dough.

make the dough into 15 small balls. Lay on a floured baking sheet and flatten to a thickness of ¼ inch.

press a blanched almond into the center of each cookie and brush with the egg-and-water mixture.

bake the cookies in a preheated oven at 350°F for 15 minutes, or until they are light brown.

lift on to a wire rack to cool.

Makes 15 biscuits
Preparation time: *15 minutes*
Cooking time: *15 minutes*
Oven temperature: *350°F*

Lychee Sorbet

Make this luscious sorbet when you want a cool, refreshing and pretty finish to a meal.

1 x 1-pound can lychees
½ cup granulated sugar
2 tablespoons lemon or lime juice
2 egg whites
rind of 1 lime, thinly pared, to decorate

drain the juice from the lychees into a measuring jug and make up to 1¼ cups with cold water. Pour into a saucepan and stir in the sugar. Heat gently until the sugar has dissolved, then bring to the boil. Simmer gently, without stirring, for 10 minutes, then remove from the heat. Set aside and allow to cool slightly.

purée the lychees in a blender or food processor or press through a sieve, then mix with the sugar syrup and lemon or lime juice. Pour the mixture into a shallow freezer container and place in the freezer for 1–2 hours, or until nearly frozen.

whisk the egg whites in a clean, dry bowl until fairly stiff. Cut the frozen mixture into small pieces, then work in a blender or food processor to break down the crystals. Without allowing the mixture to melt, quickly fold in the whisked egg white until evenly incorporated, then pour into a slightly deeper freezer container. Return to the freezer for 2–3 hours or until firm.

meanwhile, prepare the decoration. Plunge the lime rind into a saucepan of boiling water and blanch for 2 minutes. Drain, refresh under cold running water, then pat dry with absorbent paper towels, and cut into thin strips.

to serve the sorbet, remove from the freezer 10 minutes before serving. Scoop the sorbet into individual glass dishes and sprinkle with the lime rind. Serve immediately.

Serves 6
Preparation time: *30 minutes, plus 3–5 hours freezing*
Cooking time: *10 minutes*

Dim sum

Pork dim sum

Jumbo shrimp dumpling

Pork and shark fin dumpling

Steamed dumpling

Pork dim sum

The term "dim sum" encompasses a wide range of little snacks and light meals popular throughout China. They have been served for generations in Chinese tea-houses, and can also be made at home. A literal translation of dim sum means "touch the heart" which indicates the affection with which these delicious tidbits and savory morsels are regarded. The custom is to sample many kinds of different tastes and textures in tiny portions. At the same time, vast quantities of steaming hot tea are consumed — this is really necessary, because some dim sum can be very rich, and the tea aids digestion. In Chinese communities, whole families gather on Sunday mornings and enjoy their gossip and *yum cha*, which means "drink tea." Dim sum are served as a speciality on the menu of many Chinese restaurants. A wide selection is brought to the table in a special cart with heated compartments. The diners choose their favorites from the cart selection, which is frequently replenished.

Pork and shark fin dumpling

This dumpling is deep-fried and contains morsels of pork and shark's fin. Shark fin is very much sought after in China, and as a consequence it is very expensive. The delicacy is alleged to have aphrodisiac properties. The best shark's fins are found in China and the Philippines. The fins are soaked overnight and then boiled for three hours before use.

Jumbo shrimp dumpling

This dumpling is fragrant, attractive, and tastes utterly delicious! The translucent wrapper holds a pale pink filling of jumbo shrimp, fresh ginger, water chestnut, and coriander (cilantro.) The

Pork, shrimp, and egg dumpling

Char sui bao

Won ton

dumpling is steamed over a bamboo steamer and is usually served with soy sauce or chili oil for dipping.

Steamed pork dumpling

Steamed dumplings are very popular in China. To make the filling, ground pork is combined with soy sauce, ginger, and Chinese wine.

The filling is divided between flat dough circles, which are each gathered up into a package and steamed. The dumplings are served hot with a sweet-and-sour sauce.

Char sui bao

This steamed pork bun is one of the most popular types of the dim sum selection. The filling

consists of barbecued pork, red bean curd, soy sauce, onion,ginger, and garlic. Pieces of a special bread dough are wrapped around the filling and the buns are then steamed until cooked.

Pork, shrimp, and egg dumpling

The pork, shrimp, and egg mixture is placed in the center of a round noodle

wrapper, which is gathered up into a nest-shape with an open top. The dumpling is then deep fried, and served hot with a chili or soy sauce dip.

Wonton

The wonton is probably the best known of the dim sum selection. To make wontons you need wonton skins. These are rather difficult to

make at home, unless you are experienced. This need not deter you from making your own wonton, as ready-made skins are available at Chinese food markets. The skin is folded over a stuffing, usually seasoned ground pork. These are then deep-fried until they are crisp and golden. Wonton are usually served with sweet- and-sour sauce.

Breads and Pancakes

Pancake Rolls
with chicken and mushrooms

Pancake batter

2 cups all-purpose flour

pinch of salt

I egg

about I¼ cups water

Filling

I tablespoon oil

I teaspoon chopped root ginger,

2 garlic cloves, crushed

I cup skinned and diced chicken breast

2 tablespoons soy sauce

I tablespoon Chinese wine or dry sherry

I cup mushrooms, sliced

3 green onions (scallions), chopped

¼ cup peeled shrimp

sift the flour and salt into a bowl, add the egg, and beat in sufficient water to make a smooth batter.

lightly oil an 8-inch skillet and place over moderate heat. When the pan is very hot, pour in just enough batter to cover the bottom thinly, tilting the skillet to spread it evenly. Cook the pancake for 30 seconds or until the underside is just firm, then carefully remove from the pan. Repeat with the remaining batter — it should make about 12 pancakes. Keep the pancakes warm while making the filling.

make the filling: heat the oil in a wok or skillet, add the ginger, and garlic, and fry for 30 seconds. Add the chicken and brown quickly.

stir in the soy sauce and wine or sherry, then the mushrooms and green onions (scallions). Increase the heat and cook for 1 minute.

remove from the heat, stir in the shrimp, and cool.

place 2–3 tablespoons of the filling in the center of each pancake. Fold in the sides and form into a tight roll, sealing the edge with a little flour and water paste.

deep-fry the rolls a few at a time for 2–3 minutes. Drain on absorbent paper towels, then serve hot, with soy sauce as a dip, if liked.

Serves 4–6
Preparation time: *10 minutes*
Cooking time: *45 minutes*

clipboard: The chicken in this recipe could be replaced with shredded cooked pork, beef, or turkey.

Stuffed Pancakes
filled with sweet bean paste

Pancake batter
2 cups all-purpose flour
1 egg, beaten
1¼ cups water

Filling
6–8 tablespoons sweet red bean paste
or dates, finely chopped
vegetable oil, for deep-frying

put the flour into a large bowl, make a well in the center, and add the egg. Add the water gradually, beating constantly, to make a smooth batter.

lightly oil a 7-inch skillet and place over moderate heat. When the pan is very hot, pour in just enough batter to cover the bottom thinly, tilting the pan to spread it evenly.

cook for 30 seconds or until the underside is just firm, then carefully remove from the pan. Repeat with the remaining batter — it should make about 12 pancakes.

divide the sweet red bean paste or dates equally between the pancakes, placing it in the center of the uncooked side of each one.

fold the bottom edge over the filling, then fold the sides toward the center, to form an envelope. Brush the edge of the top flap with a little water, fold down, and press the edges together firmly to seal.

heat the oil in a deep-fat fryer and fry the pancakes for 1 minute or until crisp and golden. Remove and drain on absorbent paper towels. Cut each pancake into 6 or 8 slices. Serve hot, with Chinese tea.

Serves 4–6
Preparation time: *20 minutes*
Cooking time: *15–20 minutes*

clipboard: Sweet bean paste is a thick soybean paste sold in cans in Chinese food stores. It is often used as a base for sweet sauces.

Mandarin Pancakes

These are the traditional pancakes served with Peking Duck.

4 cups all-purpose flour
1¼ cups boiling water
1 tablespoon vegetable oil
3 tablespoons sesame oil

sift the flour into a mixing bowl and make a well in the center. Mix together the water and oil and gradually stir into the flour, using chopsticks or a wooden spoon. Turn the dough on to a floured worktop and knead until firm. Let the dough rest for 10 minutes.

divide the dough into 3 and roll each piece into a cylinder or finger-shape about 2 inches in diameter. Cut each one into 8. Roll the small pieces to thin, flat pancakes about 7-inches in diameter. Brush one side of half the pancakes with sesame oil. Sandwich them together with the remaining pancakes.

set a heavy skillet over a high heat without any fat. When the pan is hot, reduce the heat to moderate. Fry one pancake "sandwich" at a time, turning it over when it starts to rise and bubble, and when small brown spots appear on the underside.

when both sides are done, gently peel the 2 pancakes apart and fold each one in half, oiled side inward. Cook the remaining pancakes in the same way, keeping them warm in a low oven as the rest are cooked.

Makes 24 pancakes
Preparation time: *20 minutes, plus 10 minutes resting*
Cooking time: *about 15–20 minutes*

clipboard: The recipe for Peking Duck is on page 92. These pancakes can be made in advance, wrapped in a clean linen cloth, and reheated in a low oven when needed.

Spring Rolls
with chicken and crab

Filling

2 ounces cellophane noodles, soaked in water for
10 minutes and cut into 1-inch pieces
1 pound chicken breast meat, cut into thin strips
2 tablespoons dried wood ears (cloud ears) (see
page 192) soaked in warm water for 20 minutes
and finely chopped
3 garlic cloves, finely chopped
3 shallots, finely chopped
1 cup crabmeat
sunflower oil, for deep-frying
pepper

For the wrappers

4 eggs, beaten
20 spring roll wrappers

To garnish

green onion (scallion) tassels, to
garnish (see page 62)

make the filling: put the ingredients in a bowl and mix well. Divide into 20 portions and shape into small cylinder or finger shapes.

brush beaten egg over the entire surface of each spring roll wrapper. Leave for a few minutes until soft.

place the filling along the curved edge of the spring roll wrapper, roll once, then fold over the sides to enclose and continue rolling.

heat the oil to 350°F, or until a cube of day-old bread browns in 45 seconds. Fry the spring rolls, 5 or 6 at a time, until golden all over.

drain well on absorbent paper towels. Serve hot or warm, garnished with green onion (scallion) tassels.

Makes 20
Preparation time: *30 minutes*
Cooking time: *about 10 minutes*

clipboard: Spring roll wrappers are specially designed for this purpose and are sold in Chinese food stores. If you are unable to obtain them, use frozen filo pastry instead, cut into squares. Defrost the pastry and use it according to the packet instructions.

Shrimp Toasts
with ham and sesame seeds

*These crunchy toasts have a superb flavor — they are
a delicious snack in their own right, or can be served
as part of a Chinese meal.*

1 teaspoon Chinese wine or dry sherry
1 teaspoon salt
1 egg white
1 teaspoon cornstarch
2 cups shrimp, shelled, deveined
and finely chopped
7 slices of white bread from a large sliced
loaf, with the crusts removed
2 tablespoons sesame seeds
2 tablespoons cooked ham, chopped
oil, for deep frying
parsley sprigs, to garnish

place the wine or sherry, salt, egg white, and cornstarch in a bowl and
mix until smooth. Stir in the shrimp.

divide this mixture between the bread slices.

sprinkle with the sesame seeds and ham and press the topping firmly
into the bread, using the back of a spoon.

heat the oil to 350°F or until a cube of day-old bread browns in 45
seconds. Deep-fry the toasts, a few at a time, with the shrimp-covered side
facing downward.

when the edges of the bread turn golden, turn over on the other side.
Fry until golden brown.

drain on absorbent paper towels and cut each slice of bread into 4
squares. Arrange on a serving plate, garnish with parsley, and serve hot.

Makes 28
Preparation time: *20 minutes*
Cooking time: *20–25 minutes*

Crab Fritters
with water chestnuts

These little fritters are ideal to serve as a party snack with drinks, as well as making a savory addition to a complete meal.

1½ cups crabmeat, finely chopped
¼ cup ground pork fat
4 water chestnuts, peeled and finely chopped
1 egg white
2 tablespoons cornstarch
1 tablespoon Chinese wine or dry sherry
sunflower oil, for deep-frying
salt and pepper

place the crabmeat in a bowl with the pork fat and water chestnuts and blend well.

add the egg white, cornstarch, salt and pepper, and wine or sherry and mix together.

heat the oil in a wok or pan to 350°F, or until a cube of day-old bread browns in 45 seconds.

using a teaspoon, scoop up 1 spoonful of the crab mixture at a time and lower it into the hot oil.

fry the balls until they are golden brown, remove with a slotted spoon, and drain on absorbent paper towels.

they should be crisp on the outside and tender inside. Serve hot.

Serves 4
Preparation time: *about 30 minutes*
Cooking time: *15–20 minutes*

clipboard: Deep-frying is a popular Chinese cooking technique, used here to cook these fritters.

Dumplings
with pork and shrimp

Dough

4 cups all-purpose flour

¾ cup boiling water

½ cup cold water

Filling

2 cups lean ground pork

2 cups peeled, chopped shrimp

½ cup minced green onion (scallion)

1 tablespoon root ginger, shredded

1 tablespoon light soy sauce

1½ teaspoons salt

freshly ground black pepper

1 bunch watercress, coarsely chopped

5½ tablespoons sunflower oil

Dip

2 tablespoons wine vinegar

2 tablespoons soy sauce

make the dough: place the flour in a bowl with the boiling water. Beat well until smooth. Leave to rest for 2–3 minutes. Add the cold water and knead well.

make the filling: mix together the pork, shrimp, green onion (scallion), ginger, soy sauce, salt and pepper. Add the chopped watercress and 1 tablespoon of the oil. Blend well together.

roll the dough into a long cylinder, and slice into 1½-inch lengths. Roll each one flat to make small pancake shapes. Place 1 tablespoon of stuffing on each pancake then fold in half. Pinch the edges together to close firmly.

heat a wok and place 3 tablespoons of oil in it. Tilt the wok several times until the surface is evenly oiled. Arrange the dumplings evenly over the surface of the pan. Turn the heat to high and shallow-fry for 2–3 minutes to brown the underside of the dumplings.

add ½ cup water to the wok and cover. Steam the dumplings over high heat until almost all the water has evaporated. Remove the cover and pour in 1½ tablespoons of hot oil from the side. Reduce the heat and cook until all the liquid has evaporated.

mix the wine vinegar and soy sauce together to make a dipping sauce.

Serves 4–6
Preparation time: *20 minutes, plus 2–3 minutes resting*
Cooking time: *10-12 minutes*

Meat Dumplings
with pork and ginger

Dough

4 cups all-purpose flour
4 teaspoons baking powder
1 cup water

Filling

2 cups lean ground pork
1 tablespoon Chinese wine or dry sherry
3 tablespoons light soy sauce
2 teaspoons sugar
1 teaspoon salt
1 tablespoon sesame oil
2 teaspoons minced fresh root ginger
1 teaspoon cornstarch

sift together the flour and baking powder into a bowl. Add the water and knead well.

cover with a damp cloth and place a small plate on top. Leave the dough to rise for 2 hours.

combine the pork with the wine or sherry, soy sauce, sugar, salt, sesame oil, ginger, and cornstarch.

divide the dough in half. Knead lightly and roll each half into a sausage shape 2-inches in diameter.

divide each into about 15 rounds. Flatten the rounds, then roll out to make circles 3-inches in diameter.

place a tablespoon of filling on each circle. Gather up the sides of the dough to meet at the top, and twist to seal tightly.

arrange the dumplings ½-inch apart on a piece of damp cheesecloth in a steamer. Cover and steam vigorously for 20 minutes.

drain, if necessary, and serve hot.

Serves 4
Preparation time: *30 minutes, plus 2 hours rising*
Cooking time: *20 minutes*

Crispy Wonton
with sweet-and-sour sauce

1 pound wonton skins

3 tablespoons light soy sauce

1 tablespoon Chinese wine or dry sherry

2 cups lean ground pork

1 teaspoon brown sugar

1 garlic clove, crushed

1 x 1-inch piece fresh root ginger, peeled and finely chopped

2 cups frozen leaf spinach, thawed

sunflower oil, for deep-frying

Sauce

2 garlic cloves, crushed

1 tablespoon sunflower oil

2 tablespoons light soy sauce

2 tablespoons clear honey

2 tablespoons wine vinegar

2 tablespoons tomato paste

2 teaspoons chili sauce

2 tablespoons Chinese wine

2 teaspoons of a thin cornstarch-and-water paste

cut out 2-inch squares from the wonton skins. Put the soy sauce, sherry, and pork in a bowl and mix well.

add the sugar, garlic, and ginger. Squeeze excess liquid from the spinach in a clean cloth, and add to the mixture. Combine well.

spoon 1 tablespoon of the mixture on to the center of each wonton. Dampen the edges and fold to form triangles, pressing the edges together firmly so that the filling does not escape during frying.

heat the oil to 350°F or until a cube of day-old bread browns in 45 seconds.

fry the wonton, a few at a time, for about 5 minutes, until golden. Drain on absorbent paper towels.

make the sauce: stir-fry the garlic in the sunflower oil. Add all of the other ingredients. Bring to the boil, and cook for 2 minutes. Serve the wonton hot with the sweet-and-sour sauce.

Serves 4–6
Preparation time: *20 minutes*
Cooking time: *about 20 minutes*

clipboard: Wonton skins are made from a thin yellow dough, ready-packed in cellophane. You can buy them from Chinese food stores. Wonton are usually served as part of an assortment of *dim sum*, or afternoon snacks, in Chinese teahouses.

Index

Acknowledgments

Photo Credits
Jean Cazals: front jacket
Jean Cazals: back jacket, front flap, back flap

Special photography by Jean Cazals

All other photos:
Reed Books Ltd./William Adams-Lingwood, Bryce Attwell, Robert Golden, Melvyn Grey,
Christine Hanscomb, Tim Imrie, David Johnson, Paul Kemp, Graham Kirk, Vernon Morgan,
James Murphy, Peter Myers, Ian O'Leary, Paul Williams.

Home economist
Marie-Ange Lapierre

American adaptation
American Pie, London and Santa Clara